Growing Up Cold

A memoir of growing up cold,
but longing to be *cool*,
in 1950s Vermont

by Lucille Maurice Maistros

PublishAmerica
Baltimore

First printing

ISBN: 1-4137-5146-6
PUBLISHED BY PUBLISHAMERICA, LLLP
www.publishamerica.com
Baltimore

Printed in the United States of America

This book is dedicated to my parents,
Claire and Jimmy,
who showed me what love looked like
so I would know it when I found it.

ACKNOWLEDGMENTS

First, thank you to my best friend and husband, Chris, for his support of my writing and of all my other dreams. Your enthusiasm for this project kept me going through many moments of panic and doubt.

To Costa, my "son," thank you for designing just the cover I had in mind. Thank you to my mentor, author Les Picker, for sharing your knowledge and experience.

And to my sister and brothers, my dear family and friends, all those hours spent telling stories around the old kitchen table were the inspiration for this book. Thanks for the memories.

Although the stories are true, some names and situations have been changed and are not intended to resemble any specific persons or events. This was written in fun—I hope you will enjoy it in the same spirit.

Lucille Maurice Maistros
August 2004

INTRODUCTION

I grew up in northern Vermont, in a place called the Northeast Kingdom, a place you could spend the first twenty years of your life trying to escape, and the rest of your life trying to get back to.

I was 21 years old before I learned that most of the people in the world don't need a *summer* coat.

This is a story of growing up during the Cold War, in a cold climate—and wanting, above all, to be *cool*, but it's hard to be cool when you're a klutz and built like Kate Smith.

JANUARY

Dad's Cold War Part I – Assault on a High Ground

It was clear that my parents had not bought our house in the winter, clinging as it was to the side of Mountain Avenue, a street so steep that, even in summer, men came from all over to test their brakes driving down our street. Once they had skidded to a stop at the bottom, they would turn their cars around and drive back up again, their tires spitting sand and gravel from under the fenders. We could have sold bumper stickers, like the ones for Mount Washington: *this car climbed Mountain Avenue*.

But winter…*winter*, now that's when the fun began. We learned at a young age not to dawdle under the eaves, where icicles dangled menacingly from the edges of the roof. They would drip and grow longer during the January thaw, then freeze again into icy skirts that brushed the tops of the snow banks all around the house. And despite a day or two of warming in January, the snow would just keep coming. And coming. You could shovel every day, as we did, lifting and heaving huge shovels' full onto the sides of the driveway, until the driveway was a car-sized Luge—the surface never entirely snow-free and the walls iced-over canyons.

When it came to the challenges of Mountain Avenue, my father was no different than other men, if anything even more determined to get his car in our driveway, no matter what. One afternoon, the first winter Dad had the 1959 Chrysler Windsor with the tailfins, my brothers and I stood waiting for him to come home. It was dusk, about 4 o'clock. We were finished shoveling, cold and tired, and supper was almost ready, but we had to watch Dad come home.

As any Vermonter will tell you, there is an art to driving uphill in the winter: if you apply too much gas, your tires will spin and you won't go anywhere. Any hesitation, however, and your car will sense it, like a willful mule, the rear end will balk, smacking into anything around it. It takes experience. It takes a standard shift. And it takes a determined man like my father. Although the Chrysler was an automatic, Dad knew how to tease the transmission from *Low* to *Drive*. In the age before SUVs, he was a man who could drive *any* car *any* place.

On this particular day, though, he wasn't having any luck. It had been snowing since he had left for work that morning and the street under the new-fallen snow was slick. Crawling through powder up over the tires, the car swam all over the place, once or twice just missing the stone wall under the lilac bushes. Finally, he stopped at the bottom of the hill, climbed out of the car and opened the trunk. He stood there for a minute, in those big black rubber galoshes unbuckled over his work shoes, a red plaid wool jacket, and a gray, billed cap pulled low over his forehead, pondered for a minute or two, hands on hips, and then motioned for us to come down. We ran. "Sit in the trunk," he ordered when we slid to a stop, "put some weight on those rear tires." Then he settled himself back in behind the wheel.

You couldn't do anything in this neighborhood without attracting a crowd. In a moment, a half dozen other kids had climbed into the trunk with us. Most of them were Voisins who lived next door to us and with fourteen kids were the largest Catholic family in Scotia County. Today, using kids as trunk ballast would elicit a barrage of editorials and horrified letters asking what kind of man would risk children's lives this way. But this was a time when everyone smoked, ate fried food and drove without seatbelts. Life was an adventure.

12

After we were all settled in the open trunk, our legs dangling between the tailfins like an octopus rear-ending a killer whale, Dad slammed the car door and revved up those 450 horses for one last go. The Madonna on the dashboard trembled as the Chrysler started to lumber up the street, now as sure-footed as a Sherman tank. He kept his foot on the gas and we were moving so fast when he hit the driveway that we almost overshot the end of it—he hit the brakes before we mowed down the stand of pine trees just beyond.

The smell of burning rubber. The whine of spinning tires. Winter didn't get much better than this.

Top Ten Hints for Getting Your Car Through a Vermont Winter

10. Bring the battery indoors. A battery loses its charge as it cools. Bring it in the house, keep it warm overnight and put it back in the car in the morning.

9. Use a lamp: If you don't care to bring the battery indoors, then plug in a lamp, remove the shade, and stick it under the hood near the battery. The light bulb will keep the battery warm enough to maintain a charge.

8. Boot strapping: Old-timers tell about connecting both ends of jumper cables to the battery, which causes a chemical reaction to keep the battery charged. This can, however, cause the battery to blow up and so is no longer recommended.

7. Keep a full tank of gas. Joe Voisin learned the importance of this the time he drove his mother to the train one frigid January morning and left his Jeep running in the parking lot while he escorted her to a seat. As he got her settled in for the trip, the train lurched and began to accelerate. By the time Bobby got to the door, it was going too fast for him to jump off. He rode with his mother to White River Junction, a good hour's drive by car. Then took a cab back to town to find that his car, wreathed in a fog of its own exhaust, was still running.

6. Get a job working construction. You'll be laid off every fall and won't have to worry about your car starting from November to May.

5. Spray a thin coat of motor oil on the underside of the car. You might get two winters out of the car before road salt starts to eat holes in the frame.

4. When you park the car in the yard overnight, face it away from the direction of the wind to avoid the effects of wind chill on the cooling engine.

3. Drain the radiator overnight. A trick my grandfather used, pre-antifreeze times. Then put the water back in the morning.

2. Keep three or four extra cars lying around the yard. If you have a tendency to let cars pile up in your yard, there's a good chance that one of them will start.

1. Take the car to Florida.

Vermonters and Thermometers

Did a Vermonter invent the thermometer? Well, it should have been, but it was Daniel Fahrenheit, a Pole living in the Netherlands, who invented the mercury thermometer in 1714.

My father typified our obsession with the weather. Most mornings at sunrise, while the coffee percolated in the aluminum pot on the stove, my father stood at the kitchen window that overlooked the yard and peered out at the thermometer on the back porch. After my mother had poured him a steaming mug, he studied the movement of trees in the wind, or the body language of birds. Then he would open the back door to feel the air on his skin, the best thermal gauge. In January or February, when the red mercury had all but disappeared at the bottom of the glass tube, it would take a few minutes to get a true reading—there was always the wind chill to consider as he watched wind-made snowballs skitter across the snow-shrouded yard.

A stranger might have gotten the impression that, with all this investigation and analysis, we could actually *do* something about the weather. Or that maybe we should just move to Florida.

Born Cold, but Not *Cool*

I was born just before sunrise on a cold morning in 1948, almost at the St. Froid Police Station. Not because my parents were felons, but because typically for a January morning in the Northeast Kingdom, it was snowing like hell.

Like everything else in our town, the hospital was at the top of a hill. My father was an experienced driver, but while my mother lay across the backseat of my grandfather's 1946 Buick and tried to keep me from being born, the car continued to skate backwards down snow-covered Northern Avenue. Barely able to see through the wipers swatting at the white kaleidoscope of big white flakes, he was about to give up and pull into the police station, trusting that they knew how to deliver a baby, when, like birth itself, one more try got us up the hill to the hospital.

Had I known what the weather was like that morning, I would not have been in such a hurry. However, I didn't have a thermometer.

Can You be Cool
in Catholic School?

Our parish supported two Catholic schools, one for the boys and one for the girls, but there was never enough money for school busses. It was therefore impossible for me to look *cool* when I got to school. I arrived at Mount Saint Helene's on winter mornings like a New England boiled dinner: beet red and steaming hot, my jumper wrinkled from being tucked inside the navy-blue wool snowsuit, the pants so thick that my thighs tripped each other and I fell down a lot. Under the jumper, the white blouse that my mother had ironed was glued to my back with perspiration. A large pair of bulky wool socks went over my oxfords, which were then jammed into rubber boots. A knitted cap with a pompom was pulled down over my ears under the hood of my jacket, and my mother tied a scarf around my neck that came almost to my forehead. And, so, effectively blind and deaf, I left for school.

Sister did not stand too closely when it came time to un-bundle me in the coat closet at school. Where my hair was not mashed flat by the cap, it stood on end, crackling in a halo of static electricity.

Sister told us we should offer it up, our walk to school, for our sins, but I don't remember that I had ever done anything that bad.

It was different for some of the Catholic kids, the ones who lived on Main Street, closer to the school. In fact, you could hardly tell a Main Street Catholic from a Protestant. Some of them even got a ride to school, so they arrived fresh, their uniforms wrinkle-free, the girls' barrettes still holding their hair in place.

It just wasn't fair. *Where* you lived in our town could make the difference between being *cool* and not being *cool*.

Top Ten Things
I Thought Were Cool—1958

1. Riding to school in a bus or car
2. Shoes that don't need laces
3. Cigarettes
4. Elvis Presley
5. Sandwiches made with Wonder Bread, not homemade bread
6. Vanilla Coca Cola
7. Store-bought vs. homemade *anything*
8. Television
9. Private telephone lines
10. Whitewall tires and tail fins

Top Ten Things
I Thought Were Cool—2004

1. Walking to work
2. Reeboks
3. Not smoking
4. Frank Sinatra
5. High-fiber baguettes
6. Chardonnay
7. Home-made anything
8. Satellite radio
9. Cell phones
10. Whitewall tires and tail fins

St. Froid: A Town Divided

Can you be cool if you live on the wrong side of the river? The Oompassaic River, which was named by the native Abenakis and means *Leave this place before the snow falls*, divided our town: west from east, Main Street from River Street, and the *haves* from the *have-some-but-would-like-to-have-mores*.

The early settlers built rough cabins, a tavern, a general store, and a meetinghouse on a hilltop that overlooked the Oompassaic River valley, out of the flood plain and on one of the few flat spots east of the Winooski River. This later became Main Street, and, generations later, doctors and lawyers would live there in big Victorian houses with turrets and wrap-around porches, tucked among the gray granite churches and venerable old maples.

When the railroads came in the 1850s and stitched their tracks in the valley below, a commercial district, Depot Street, grew up along the river. The town grew substantially after that, at last more accessible to the rest of civilization. Until the trains came, it took about two weeks to get to Boston by horse or cart. With the railway, you could get your stuff there in less than a day. The railroads brought prosperity. Two brand new streets sliced down the hillside forest from Main Street to Depot Street and the riverfront. Houses went up, seemingly overnight, and neighborhoods grew and spread across the river until the bustling town had to build a second bridge to connect the two sides. Years later, after the flood of 1927 when the old wooden structure was lost, a colossal two-lane overpass of concrete and steel was built, soaring high over the river, the tallest structure in St. Froid that wasn't a church.

And that's where we lived: on the other side of that overpass. Across the overpass and up the tree-shaded sidewalk of River Street was our neighborhood, not as grand as Main Street, but because of its location along the east side of the Oompassaic River, a lot of fun to grow up in.

In St. Froid, the other side of the river did not mean the other side of the tracks.

The Other Side of the River

On the edge of town, where the paved streets met the unpaved county roads, our neighborhood was the kind where my mother could pin a check on the clothesline on the back porch for the insurance man, and it would stay there unmolested, snapping in the breeze next to the dishtowels, until he came by to pick it up.

And although we had to walk farther to school, almost a mile, it was worth it. We could fish just a few yards from our back door with homemade poles, string and safety pins, pick pails of blackberries by the side of the dirt road, and in winter, skate down the black ice of the frozen Oompassaic River until dark.

Yet, the advantages of in-town living were just a short walk away, across the overpass: The library. The pool. Woolworth's. We had the best of both worlds.

Sex Education
in Catholic School

There *was* sex in the fifties. It had evidently been going on for years before I found out about it. It was hard to get all the facts, though. Sex Education at Notre Dame Junior High consisted of Father LaSalle's escorting the boys—snickering all the way—to another classroom to explain the facts of life, in what I heard later was graphic detail, while Sister Mary Margaret, clearing her throat and twirling her rosary beads, asked us girls if we had any questions.

Questions? How can you have questions when you don't have any idea of the topic? Although we were now in our early teens, and we girls had started our monthlies, the details of the whole baby-making process were still pretty sketchy. Our mothers had explained just what we needed to know at that moment, and not one word more. The prevailing notion at the time being that too much detail would result in rampant sexual experimentation. If we didn't know about it, we couldn't do it.

It was May. We were in eighth grade, completing our finals in academic subjects as well as our final days of relative innocence before we started high school in the fall. It was Sister's last chance to keep us from the sins of the flesh. So while the bees buzzed and the birds chirped out the open windows, we waited for Sister to clear up the mysteries: (a) how did the baby get into the mother's tummy? (b) how did it come out of the tiny opening of the belly button—did it just automatically zip open?

And then my own personal favorite question, which I had first broached to my mother in front of the prescription counter at Armand's Pharmacy when I was eleven years old. While we watched Mr. Armand, who went to our church and who my mother had known for her whole entire life, put the brown bottle of cough syrup into a white paper bag, I turned to her and asked, "Hey, Mom. Dad isn't related to me, is he?"

Mr. Armand, unflappable, having raised six children of his own, just smiled, looked over my head and thanked my mother. But I had never seen my mother move so quickly as her face reddened and she hustled me out the door.

"Of course he's related to you!" she said as we started across the overpass.

"But how?" I asked again, sincerely perplexed. "I mean—you're the one who had us—Dad didn't have anything to do with it, did he?"

"I'll tell you some other time—when you're older," she answered. And I knew better than to push her when she walked that fast.

As for my first sexual experience, I was seven and Billy Baxter had come over to color with me. He was older, about eight, I think, with red hair and freckles, cute in an Alfalfa kind of way. Mom was in the kitchen, peeling potatoes, while we sat at the dining room table. With my tongue sandwiched between my teeth, a family trait that indicates intensity, I concentrated on staying within the lines while I colored Dale Evans's fringed western shirt. Without warning, he reached under the table and groped for my crotch. I exploded from my seat, like a pilot ejecting from a cockpit, and knocked the chair over. When my mother hurried in and asked what was wrong I lied and said, "Nothing—I...I just fell out of the chair." I had to live in the same neighborhood with that kid and I didn't want to tell on him. But I never invited him over again.

When I was ten, my friend Annie filled me in on what she knew. Her mom was d-i-v-o-r-c-e-d, one of only two divorcees in our town in 1958. Annie's mom worked full time as a waitress so she wasn't home when we got home from school. On her days off, she smoked Lucky Strike cigarettes and read *True Confession* magazines that she kept on a TV tray by her chair. So, Annie had access to lots of good information about sex. One afternoon while we drank lime Fizzies in her kitchen and flipped through stories with titles like "Love in a Pup Tent" and "Punished for My Sins," Annie said, "I know how people make babies."

"You do not!" I said excitedly.

"I do so and I'll tell you, but don't tell your mother."

Of course not, besides, I figured my mother knew all about it anyways.

"Well," she began, "first, your father ties your mother to a tree…"

Gross! I thought as she continued. Clearly, she had been reading too many *True Confessions.* She was even more confused than I was.

As for having babies, I knew that God had something to do with it. But sometimes I wondered how He knew when a woman was married and that it was okay to send her a baby. Did God ever get his baby orders mixed up? Had He ever accidentally sent one to a woman a little early…*before* she got married? I was going to ask Mom about that one of these days.

So, anyways, back to the classroom on this spring day in 1962, as I sat in the back of the classroom and waited for Sister to hand over the truth, once and for all. But she droned on that (a) your body is a Holy Temple, and (b) relations between husband and wife are Holy and only happen when two people are married and really, really love each other and want to have a baby, and (c) a woman should save herself for her husband.

Save what? *That* was the question! That's what we wanted to know! We needed some solid facts: what were we supposed to protect?

We were not going to find out that day, either. Sister finished with the advice to "ask your mother" if we needed to know any more.

Then the boys filed back into class and we could tell by the looks on their faces that Father LaSalle had taken the proverbial bull by the horns. They *knew*.

After school that day, Patsy and I sat huddled in a booth at Barker's Rexall Drug Store stirring our vanilla cokes and listening as Tommy Connolly, who was just our pal and not like a *guy* guy, shared with us what Father had told them. I was shocked. So that's how Dad was related to me.

Later, while I dried the supper dishes, I asked my mother if sex was *holy*. Suds up to her elbows, she turned to Dad who had his arms around her waist, smiled and said, "Well, it's not like saying your rosary beads."

Not My Strong Suit

I thought maybe being an athlete would make me *cool*. My best friend Patsy was one of the coolest people I knew and she was a wonderful athlete; she could beat anybody, even boys, at basketball. So in eighth grade, I signed up for the basketball team.

They gave me a uniform consisting of a purple short-sleeve blouse with the number "8" on the back, and a box-pleated skirt attached to a pair of purple bloomers. I looked like the awning in front of the St. Froid Fruit Market.

I attended all the practices in the hope that with this much exercise I'd carve out the body I had always wanted: long and lean. After weeks of after-school practice, Coach Carter—a big guy with the obligatory John Wayne swagger whose day job was selling Ford pickups—actually did put me into the game a few times, but probably more as a favor to my father. But, invariably, before the end of the first quarter, the eighth grade's all-star athletes Patsy and Marcie would have to carry me off the court with a sprained ankle where I would spend the rest of the game on the bench with an ice pack.

In the end, my only contribution to our athletic success was to steal the Notre Dame Victory Song from that college out in Indiana and adapt it for our use. Now *that's* what I was good at: it involved music, not running around chasing a ball.

Airborne

Kids are always coming up with ingenious new ways to hurt themselves. It is a wonder that we manage to grow up at all. Even in a town like St Froid, as placid as a porch swing, and in a school like Mount St. Helene's, you could get into a lot of trouble. Trust me.

There was the incident when I was twelve involving the glass door in the girls' bathroom. I wasn't *trying* to break it; my fist was aimed at Roxanne Genovese—in fun—when she tried to stop the punch with the door. They took me to the Foley Clinic and it took twelve stitches to fix my hand. And then Dad spent one of his precious Saturday afternoons repairing the glass, nuns bobbing and tittering around him the whole time, unable, despite their vows, to resist his charm.

And then there was the time in the spring of 1961 when I was thirteen that we almost killed Katy. It wasn't all my fault, really. I would rather have been home that blustery April afternoon eating chocolate chips straight from the yellow bag, with a chaser of marshmallow fluff, but I was, instead, being punished after school for—big surprise—talking in class. This time my three best friends, Katy, Annie and Patsy, were there with me for another serious infraction—passing notes in class.

Sister Agatha's favorite punishment was to have us copy from the encyclopedia into our black marble copybooks. This way we were killing two birds: learning discipline and learning something from the encyclopedia. But there is one heckuva lot of small print on one page of the Encyclopedia Britannica. My hand still cramps at the memory.

And Sister did not want us to scribble—the writing must be legible. But even when I was careful, my penmanship was barely legible, a trait I had inherited from my father. To make matters worse, back in second grade, seeking self-expression in a world of strict order and uniforms, I had decided to personalize my handwriting by leaving off all the "tails" that finish the letters. This, however, made it difficult to connect letters smoothly to one another to form words; each letter just sort of stood there, arms at its sides, looking lonely and sheepish.

By late afternoon on this April day, when the oak grandfather's clock in the hall next to Our Lady's statue chimed 4 o'clock, we had all finished our copying, except for Katy. She was a methodical person who could not be rushed. There she still sat, in deep concentration, when Sister said the rest of us could go home. But we didn't want to leave without Katy. So, we gathered up our books, went outside and waited for her in front of the convent.

I suggested that we kill time by checking out the list of movies that had been banned by The Legion of Decency and that Father LaSalle posted in the vestibule of the church. Titles like *Baby Doll* and *And God Created Woman* made you wonder what all the fuss was about but it was, after all, forbidden fruit and so we were curious. But this day, we decided to stay put and wait for Katy.

It was a gray, overcast April day—spring had arrived, sort of. We stood in the weak, watery sunshine, our knees above our knee socks red and chapped from the wind, and waited. Just as we were about to give up, there she stood, Katy, waving from the second-story window. She opened the window and called to us in a loud whisper that Sister Agatha had left to check on something.

"So leave!" I called to her, now growing concerned at how late it was. Dad would be home from Saxon's Wagon and Tool Works by now and Mom would have supper on the table promptly at five o'clock—no martinis and hors d'oeuvres in *this* town. We had to get

Katy out of there and go home. But Katy said no, she was already in enough trouble. And besides, Sister had locked the door.

"So jump out the window!" somebody yelled. I don't think it was me, but Annie and Patsy insist that I was the one who started it. Anyway, before I knew it, things were getting serious.

"Go ahead, *jump!* We'll catch you! Just throw your books out first."

Katy, like me, had never met a doughnut she didn't like; she would not have been an easy catch. Patsy was the athlete and had big muscles for a girl, but Annie was super skinny and most likely couldn't catch anything but a cold. Before we could change our minds, here came all of Katy's things—loose-leaf binder, Baltimore Catechism, textbook of American History—sailing out the window, the binder open and scattering blue-inked mimeographed homework sheets all over the convent yard, wind-whipped in the bluster, like a ticker-tape parade. And then there's Katy and she's already got one chubby thigh dangling over the windowsill.

Katy always insisted that she would have jumped that day. We'll never really know. Suddenly, a dark shadow loomed over Katy's shoulder.

"What do you think you're doing!" Sister shouted, bringing the whole near-catastrophe to a halt. Sister stood there for a couple of minutes, her mouth moving but nothing coming out, and finally told Katy to go. "Out the *door!* Out the *door!*" we could hear her from the yard.

So, no harm was done after all, except some of Katy's papers were smudged from the dampness in the convent yard. It was, however, my first introduction to the mob mentality, and I learned that people would do things in a crowd that they wouldn't do alone. It was pretty scary.

Growing Up Ozzie & Harriet in a Castro & Khrushchev World

It's hard to learn anything in school when you spend most of the day on your knees, under your desk, staring at the backside of the kid in front of you. This was because of *the bomb*. Is it any wonder that *we* were the generation who spawned the sixties revolution? How can you grow up normal in an era that is defined on one hand by threats of annihilation and on the other by Howdy Doody?

Thanks to the air-raid drills, we were ready for *the bomb*. But because of the transitional culture of the fifties, we were not as well prepared for some of the other gritty realities of life we would have to face in another time, another place. Our parents were confused, too, giving us conflicting messages: don't follow the crowd (if Johnny jumped off the overpass, would *you* jump off the overpass?) but *do* worry about what the neighbors think. Go to college and make something of yourself, but don't leave home. Good girls look like Donna Reed, but women who look like Marilyn Monroe get asked out. We were a naïve and bewildered generation.

And we worried. We worried about things like:

- The *bomb*
- What kind of winter did the *Old Farmers' Almanac* predict for northern New England?
- The *bomb*
- Would the Red Sox get into the World Series?
- And—the *bomb*

Besides the *bomb*, we Catholic kids had to worry about mortal sin and going to hell. A potpourri of horror stories merged in our imaginations to keep us awake on those long arctic January nights as we tossed in our flannel pajamas, visions of the gruesome martyr stories we'd heard in catechism projected in 3-D on the insides of our eyelids. *Glorious martyrdom* they called it, such as Saint Lawrence who was fried on a griddle. "Turn me over, I'm done on this side," he had supposedly called to his torturers. And there was young Maria Goretti, stabbed to death rather than yield her virginity—although we didn't know what *that* was.

Somehow I knew, in the deep dark recesses of my frightened little Catholic heart, that if the Russians ever conquered New England *and* managed to find their way through the great forests of central Maine to St. Froid *and* demanded that I renounce my faith, I would have to say, "*What* faith?"

Martyrdom? A polio vaccination was suffering enough.

Sometimes hiding under the desk was a good idea.

Segregation—Yankee Style

There was segregation in our town, but of a different sort than you'd find in Birmingham or Yazoo City. After all, you're not likely to have a lot of bigotry in a town with only one black family, and they so light that most people didn't know they were black and wouldn't have cared anyway.

Our segregation was carved, instead, along religious lines. We Catholics were segregated from the Protestants, and then sub-segregated again into two Catholic parishes: St. Patrick's, the Irish Church, and Notre Dame des Neiges (Our Lady of the Snows), the French Church. There were other ethnic groups that attended the Irish Church, but whether they spoke with an Irish Brogue or an Italian accent, what they shared was that they sure as heck didn't speak French. And at Notre Dame, like it or not, the mass was in Latin and French. Although the French sermon was sometimes repeated in English, it was still foreign enough that the English-speakers wanted no part of it.

When I was seven, we lived on Spring Street, about six blocks from Notre Dame. On nice Sunday mornings, my father would leave the DeSoto parked under the trees in front of the house and we would walk to mass. On the way, we passed the smaller brick church of St. Patrick.

"Why can't we go to this church?" I asked my father one Sunday morning as he steered me along the sidewalk. It was just the two of us—Mom had gone to an earlier mass and was home with the boys.

"It's the Irish Church," he said. "And we go to the French church."

Okay, then. That was enough for me. I didn't know if that meant the devil himself would come out and drag us down the sidewalk if we went into that church, but you didn't argue with my father.

One Sunday, in a playful mood, Dad stopped on the sidewalk in front of St. Patrick and instead of continuing, took me by the hand, up the stairs, and into the vestibule. I was scandalized.

"But Dad, we can't go in there!" I whispered, horrified as I looked at the backs of the people in their pews. The people looked normal enough. I even recognized a couple of kids from school.

"It's okay," he said, "this is a Catholic church, too. We can hear mass here for a change."

Thus it was: the complete separation of the two parishes until an unseasonably warm Saturday in November 1966, when a young boy playing with vigil lights caused the fire that burned Notre Dame down to a rubble-filled hole in the ground.

Sometime later, after much soul-searching and, ultimately, a decision by the bishop, the two Catholic churches finally joined into one, and the two reluctant congregations learned to come together—and *pray* nice.

Ice Breaking

Despite being athletically gauche, I loved to ice skate. I loved it even though a) you had to be outside in the cold and b) my weak ankles wore out the *sides* of my skates first.

We dressed for skating in thick nylon snow pants and parkas, wool socks pulled up to our knees, knitted caps, scarves, and mittens. When the cold overwhelmed even these defenses, we climbed the steps to the skating shack and creaked open the wooden door. A cocoon of heated air drew us into that cozy little room where we sat on the benches that lined the shack and held our hands over the potbellied stove, our skates adding more slices to a floor carved into slivers by generations of skaters.

There wasn't much room in the skating shack, a good reason to sit close together. This was much appreciated as we got to be teenagers. The rink caretaker, Mr. Black, stoked the blaze inside the stove until it popped and crackled, and in that smoky room, with all those raging hormones, the smell of wood smoke became as alluring to me as the scent of King's Men aftershave.

In the end, besides those moments of bundled intimacy, I guess I liked skating so much because it was like anything else that was challenging and uncomfortable—it felt so good when you stopped.

St. Froid: A Small Town with Big Ideas

St. Froid was not a big town, but it had big-town ideas. We didn't have to live in Boston to enjoy certain amenities.

According to a St. Froid Town Directory published in 1952, the 8,000 people in St. Froid were served by twelve churches, eleven beauty salons, ten barbershops, nine shoe stores, eight clothing stores, seven taverns, four railroad lines, two piano tuners, and one traffic light.

There were two hospitals: one Catholic and one Protestant. Two funeral homes: one Catholic and one Protestant. And two cemeteries: one Catholic and one Protestant.

And yet, in a community of this size, with a humble tax base of about 2500 employed adults, there was a daily newspaper, the *St. Froid Times* (*All of the news some of the time; some of the news all of the time*), paid, full-time fire department and police departments, maintenance and snow removal crews, weekly garbage collection, and a town dump. In 1934, not to be left behind at the dawn of air travel, the people voted at Town Meeting to build an airport, the St. Froid Municipal Airport, with two runways and a Quonset hut-style hangar. They built the runways long enough to land bombers, thinking it is better to anticipate expansion rather than to start too small.

Just down Route 5, only a mile or so from the airport, was a nine-hole golf course and country club—nine holes being about all you could squeeze in without having a coronary from climbing the hills.

And there were schools—nine in all. If you left St. Froid uneducated, it was not for lack of opportunity. Heading the list was the private St. Froid Academy Preparatory High School. The town paid our tuition if we chose to go there, we blue collar children rubbing elbows with the boarding students, children of affluent families from exotic places like Long Island and Boston. "Why," I wondered back then, ignorant of the great, wide world, "would any kid *want* to come to this hick town to go to school?"

And the town fathers did not forget those less fortunate, the indigent and handicapped, who lived and earned their keep at The Town Farm.

Our town even boasted a museum of natural science, an art gallery, and my favorite place—the library, perched at the head of Main Street and crammed to its Victorian medallion-plastered ceiling with books, books, books. All three of these facilities had been donated to the townspeople by Orville and Wilbur Saxon, founders of Saxon's Wagon and Tool Works, who felt that a cultured and entertained workforce was a contented workforce. They were right.

A Little Family Background

We were Canucks. My father was born in a small town in Quebec and my mother's family had also originated from there. Our ancestors had emigrated from mild, temperate Normandy in the mid-seventeenth century to settle on the frigid, snow-swept plains of eastern Quebec, which gives you an idea of just how bad things were in France at the time.

Judging by my relatives, our Norman ancestors were warm and friendly folks who loved music, beer, and a good laugh.

My parents had fallen in love while performing in local musical theater. In the play *Hearts and Gowns*, they played two people who fell in love—and then they did. Like Nelson Eddy and Jeanette McDonald, whom I thought they resembled, they were good looking and their voices were beautiful. Not one of us kids inherited their voices, but their love of music is coiled like piano wire into the helix of our DNA.

I was the oldest of two girls and two boys, and thus third in the chain of command—a duty I exercised often and diligently, especially with my brother Spike who was 23 months younger than I. Ricky was four years younger, and Cissy was eleven years younger.

Dad spent World War II repairing B-29s on the island of Tinian in the Marianas. Thus, we had a more intimate connection to *the bomb* than most people: he had worked on the bomb-bay doors of the *Enola Gay* before it left for Japan on that early August morning in 1945. After return to civilian life, he worked as a machinist at the shop, as they called it, Saxon's Wagon and Tool Works.

My mother was a switchboard operator for New England Telephone and Telegraph, starting in 1940 when there were no dial phones and you had to make all calls through the operator. She was still working as an operator when we were kids and we loved knowing that we could come home from school, pick up the phone, and dial "O" and hear her voice. If another operator answered, we had only to ask to speak to her.

They were ordinary people in an ordinary place; the memories they left us, however, were anything but.

FEBRUARY

Color Me Gray

I've heard people say, who have never experienced a Vermont winter and who are trying to comprehend the subzero temperatures, "It's a different cold up north…it's a dry cold…it's not really that cold."

It was different, all right. Fingertips inside the warmest of wool mittens felt as though they'd been singed. Nostrils stuck together. Ice crystals in the air gave it a dusky blue quality and on bitter cold mornings, the houses and chimney smoke across the river looked like paintings on blue canvas. There was an eerie stillness, the cold muffling even the crash of railcars in the switchyard across the river. Now and then, you'd hear the faint jingle of chain-covered snow tires flogging the undersides of car fenders as they cautiously crunched down the street.

When temperatures went down to thirty below, relative humidity was not a big factor.

February blew us the worst of the arctic cold. Everything was gray: gray skies, gray snow, gray faces. For days, sometimes weeks, temperatures barely made it up to zero at high noon. That time of year, Dad used a heater on his car engine every night to make sure it would start in the morning. Sometimes the fear that their cars

Lucille Maurice Maistros

wouldn't start drove men to overdo it, like the time Mr. Voisin put a
blanket over the hood of his car, in addition to the engine heater, and
the blanket caught fire and melted all the hoses under the hood.

To make things even more miserable, February is stuck in a time
warp—somewhere between the merriment of Christmas and the
promise of Easter. Lent usually starts in February—we children would
have to give up something for a Lenten sacrifice. I tried to give up
parsnips, one year, but Mom said that didn't count.

The Romans were wise, old Julius and Augustus. When they were
going about stealing days from other months to make their namesake
months longer, they plundered them from February.

A Miracle for the Birds

We were the last generation born before television, and so, compared to the kids of today, we were a pretty naïve and unsophisticated bunch. Raised in a culture of mysteries and miracles, anything seemed possible—from the Easter Bunny to the Tooth Fairy.

On bitterly cold days, we crossed the river on the bridge that ran under the overpass, even though there was the risk that we could be dinged by pigeon poop. I usually tried to distract myself from the cold by planning how I would go about investigating a murder, if I ever found a body, say, down under the bridge along the riverbank. I had given up on the idea of becoming an archeologist and wanted to become a detective like Nancy Drew. My father said detectives earned more than archaeologists and that, anyway, I was better suited to be a detective—it takes a certain calm and patient temperament to be an archeologist; you can't just start rooting up artifacts with a backhoe.

When I was ten, I did find a dead body, of sorts, one frigid February afternoon after school. Spike and Ricky walked a few feet ahead of me, but they missed it, untrained as they were in detective work. It was a pigeon, lying on the sidewalk. Further investigation revealed—I nudged it with my boot—that it wasn't dead. But it was hurt and couldn't fly. I called my brothers over to look at it. Generally, everyone in St. Froid hated the pigeons that roosted under the overpass, but this attitude was apt to fade when it came up against a kid's inherent need to rescue injured wildlife. And this little bird was cute, with a tiny head and white and gray feathers. He shivered when Spike picked it up in his mittens. "We can't just leave him here," Ricky said. So, we took him home.

When we got home, Spike showed him to Mom. Although she warned us not to bring "that filthy thing into this house," she let us put him in a cardboard box on the back porch and offer him some Cheerios. The bird perched quietly on its rag bed while we, waiting for Dad to get home, watched him from the kitchen window. Dad knew everything there was to know about animals. "He's probably eaten some of that poisoned feed the town puts out to get rid of them," he said after he'd had a chance to look at him, "but we'll see."

The next morning, the temperature on the back porch was 35 degrees below zero but we couldn't wait to leave for school so we could check on our bird. When Spike pulled open the back door, there was no reaction from the bird. It was still scrunched down, much the way we'd left it the night before. Spike poked it and it fell right over, frozen stiff. We went in and told Mom. She threw on her coat, came outside, and said he did look dead, but that freezing to death is supposed to be a peaceful way to go. I don't know how anybody knows that.

We were sad. I mean, it wasn't as bad as when Minou, our cat, was killed by a car, but rescuing something creates a bond between the rescuer and the rescuee. Then I got to thinking maybe it was our fault because we had taken him away from the other birds at the bridge and he had died of a broken heart.

Later that afternoon when we got home from school, the pigeon was gone. My mother said he had thawed out and flown away. Apparently, she thought, he hadn't been frozen all the way through. But *we* knew what had really happened: a miracle.

Growing Up Cold

I was seventeen and in the middle of telling this story to a friend when my mother broke in and confessed that our bird had not thawed out and flown away: she had put on her coat and boots, taken his frozen body across the snow-covered back yard and buried him beneath the drift along the fence. She had not had the heart to tell us, during this bleakest time of the year. Instead, she had given us hope. Our own little Lazarus had arisen and flown away. With enough faith, anything was possible.

MARCH

Cabin Fever

Cabin fever is real. By March, we'd been cooped up for going on six months and we were getting mean. One year I broke Spike's favorite 78-rpm record, *Twelfth Street Rag* by the Firehouse Five plus Two. On purpose. Over his head. He retaliated by putting my favorite record, Patti Page's *How Much is That Doggie in the Window*, on my chair at the table so I'd sit on it.

My parents had also reached the end of their rope. Dad spent many a bleak evening standing at the back door, hands behind his back, peering through the frosted window at the thermometer on the back porch, just to see how low it would go. "You won't believe it," he'd turn to us, doing homework at the table, "twenty-five below and still going down." Mom would look out the window over the sink as she washed out his black metal lunch box and thermos, and you knew she was thinking about that first spring day when she'd be able to throw open the window and smell grass growing, and that if she had to spend one more day in this house she'd start packing our suitcases and ask my father to take us back to California (see October).

By March, the novelty of snow had worn off; it had, in, fact, worn off back around New Year's Day. And it was getting harder to find places to dump it. We walked carefully past the neighbors' driveways on the way to school: people backing out between huge snow banks couldn't see us and we couldn't see them either, only the smoky plumes of their car exhaust rising over the white mounds.

The only thing that redeemed that whole damn month was sugar on snow.

If you're a Vermonter, you know what I'm talking about. If you're not, then buy some real maple syrup, put it in a pot on the stove, and check out the recipe that follows.

On a Sunday afternoon in mid-March, when the icicles on the eaves had begun dripping promisingly over the back stairs, my grandparents and Aunt Aileen would come over, along with maybe Aunt Priscilla and Uncle Steve. Dad would pour a quart or two of syrup into a large pot on the stove and let it simmer until it thickened. While it simmered my mother assembled paper plates, a jar of her homemade dill pickles, and about a dozen of Grammy's doughnuts. She'd scoop out a portion of snow from a large pan and put some on each plate. The snow was clean. We had watched from the back seat of the Chrysler while my father stepped into the woods and scooped from the center of snowy remnants of storms that had fallen in December.

While we waited for the syrup to cook, Uncle Steve who lived on a farm reminded us that it takes 40 gallons of sap to make one gallon of syrup. It also takes several cords of wood and a sincere commitment to the project once the sap starts running—there's no holding it back for a couple of weeks.

It seemed to take forever to boil down to the right consistency there in our kitchen, until finally, after testing it one last time on a small plate of snow, Dad announced that it was ready. We would pass him our plates. He'd drizzle a couple of tablespoons on the snow on each plate and we'd go back to the table with our prize, by which time the syrup had toughened into a taffy that we rolled around a fork and ate with the doughnuts and dill pickles to cut the sweetness.

Sugar on snow has probably saved many a Vermonter from turning to whiskey to get through this bleak time of year—but just barely.

Sugar on Snow

♦ 1 quart of real Vermont maple syrup
♦ ½ teaspoon butter
♦ Packed snow or well-crushed ice

Heat syrup with butter, watching pot if it threatens to boil. When a candy thermometer reaches 234°, remove pot from heat and cool slightly. Test by spooning a tablespoon on the snow. If the syrup sits on top of the snow and clings to the fork like taffy, it's ready. Pour in "ribbons" over snow or crushed ice, then wrap around forks to eat. Traditionally served with plain doughnuts and sour pickles.

Maple Pudding Cake

Still don't have your fill of maple syrup flavor? This recipe should do it!

♦ 1½ cups flour (preferably unbleached)
♦ 2 tsps baking powder
♦ ¾ cup milk
♦ ¾ cup water
♦ 2 tablespoons butter
♦ ¾ cup maple or white sugar
♦ ¼ tsp salt
♦ 1½ cups Vermont maple syrup

Preheat oven to 350°

Combine flour, sugar, baking powder, and salt. Stir in milk. Spread batter in 9-inch greased baking pan or dish.

Combine syrup, water, and butter in saucepan and heat until butter is melted. Gently pour the heated liquid over batter in the pan and bake about 45 minutes until cake is lightly browned. The maple syrup mixture will sink to the bottom where it will form a pudding-like sauce. Cool briefly and top with whipped cream or ice cream.

The End of the Innocence at Mount Saint Helene

In March 1958, I discovered *Casablanca* on television one Saturday afternoon. From then on, I wanted to look like Ingrid Bergman when I grew up. But my fourth grade school picture reveals I was headed more toward Imogene Coca: bangs cut straight across the brows, a broad smile displaying a gap between two front teeth, and a big mouth—in more ways than one. I am wearing a dark navy dress patterned with orange dragonflies, short puffy sleeves, white peter-pan collar, and an orange string tie.

From my wide-eyed grin you can tell I was as trusting as a spring lamb, something that was about to change.

We were two weeks away from St. Patrick's Day and the convent's annual St. Patrick's Day bazaar when Sister Eileen made an announcement that would shock and thrill us all.

The bazaar was held each year to raise money for the little pagan babies in foreign lands. Even two weeks out, Mount St. Helene's was already plastered with paper shamrocks and cardboard cutouts of *Erin go bragh*, which Katy told me had nothing to do with Irish underwear but actually meant *Ireland Forever*. We fourth graders were hosting a beanbag toss; participants could win holy pictures and glow-in-the-dark rosary beads. We sold refreshments, even in the middle of Lent—a special dispensation from Monsignor Breton—popcorn and fudge in waxed-paper bags, Dixie cups of green Kool-Aid, and our mothers' homemade cookies. Sister Cecilia, the music teacher, would provide the Irish music on her portable Philco record player, which looked a lot like the suitcase where Edgar Bergen kept Charlie McCarthy, and the fifth grade girls in green crepe-paper skirts and white blouses would demonstrate an Irish jig.

It was a Friday afternoon, the smell of tuna still heavy in the air, when Sister announced that this year there would be something really special at the bazaar: a real, live *leprechaun*! And it would only cost a nickel to see him. Father McNally had returned from his pilgrimage to Ireland with the little man who would be staying at St. Patrick's rectory until the bazaar.

We were stunned. Did we believe it? Well, being Catholic is all about faith: having some and holding on to it. So—why not?

I told Mom and Dad all about it, Dad remarking that he wasn't surprised that Father McNally was seeing little green men after a trip to Ireland. They agreed, however, to give some money for the bazaar. My brothers wished they could see it, too, but the boys of St. Bernard's were not invited.

As for Patsy, Katy, Annie, and I, it was all we could talk about over lunch for the next two weeks, peanut butter and marshmallow-fluff sandwiches drying up on their waxed-paper wrappings as we argued about what he would look like. Katy, of course, knew best: an elf-like man with pointed ears, wearing green shorts and a hat, and smoking a pipe. Although our knowledge of baby making was sketchy, we debated whether there were girl leprechauns...else, how would you make more leprechauns?

St. Patrick's Day finally dawned with heavy gray skies and snow drifting down in a curtain of white so thick it hid even the river from view. But this was The Big Leprechaun Day. I had to get to school—snowdrifts or not. I could not miss the biggest thing to hit Mount St. Helene's since the convent drill team marched for John Phillip Sousa's visit in 1930.

The convent already smelled like popcorn when I got there—even the coatroom where we stowed our lunches on a shelf and where, by 3 o'clock, my jacket usually smelled of damp wool, bananas, and egg salad.

We had to wait until the afternoon to go to the eighth-grade classroom where the leprechaun was on display, but the four of us managed to be first in line, nickels in hand, so desperate for a glimpse that we would have gladly carried our nickels to the foreign missions ourselves, just for a peek. Since she was Irish, we let Katy go first. Sister Eileen reminded her not to tell anyone what he looked like until everyone had had a chance to see him. He was in a green felt-covered box on a small table. Katy walked over and waited while one of the eighth-grade girls opened the lid. Then she looked inside.

After what seemed like hours, she straightened, her face so red her freckles had disappeared, and scurried away, like something was about to climb up the sides of that box and come out after her. I felt that sudden rumbling of the bowels you get when you've been snooping around in your mother's bureau. When Sister Eileen asked for my nickel, I knew it was too late to run. Besides, I couldn't chicken out now. Katy had already seen it. So, I walked over and looked inside.

And there it was: my own shocked reflection looking up at me from a mirror glued to the bottom of the box. A trick! It was just a trick to get our nickels.

For the first time in my life, I was speechless. I found Katy laughing and trying not to pee herself in the coatroom. "I had to get out of there," she said, "cause I wanted to laugh and I would have given the whole thing away!"

She may have been amused but I was humiliated. Now I would have to tell my two brothers who would laugh at me as they had last Christmas when they spotted my letter to Santa on the Christmas tree. Their friends had told them there was no Santa but I hated to take a chance.

And so, for me, this was the end of the innocence at Mount Saint Helene. Everything became suspect after The Great Leprechaun Hoax of 1958.

The Yankee Law of Natural Retribution

Law #1: In spring, if you rush the season,
you'll catch pneumonia and die.

Spring, Stone Walls, and Winstons

Don't kid yourself that Vermonters built those picturesque stone walls that wander over the hills and frame the pastures like gray picture mats just to entertain tourists. The glacier was the reason. When it started to melt and recede, about 10,000 years ago, before most Vermonters were born, and crept back over what would later become the Canadian border, the rocks stayed behind, dotting the fields and pastures of the Green Mountain State and assuring that, even today, the easiest crops to grow in Vermont are cows, goats, and tourists.

Every spring, when the ground warmed and the snow melted, weary farmers would find a new crop of rocks, heaved up by the thawing earth, that they would gather, haul to the edges of their property, and dump into piles. Over generations, the walls grew along these lines, turning the pastures into art.

In the spring of 1963, I discovered other uses for those old walls. There was a stone wall on River Road, not far from our house, holding back a large embankment that had at one time been the outer edge of a Catholic cemetery. They had moved the cemetery across town about a hundred years ago, but the place where it had been abutted Mr. Voisin's garden. Red Voisin liked to tell about mysterious lights moving over that spot, and now and then, a bone would work its way up through Mr. Voisin's green peppers and string beans. Digging around one day, we found what we were convinced was a kneecap, poking through the dirt between the scallions.

I was a freshman in the spring of 1963 so it was even more important that I ditch the coat, hat, scarf, and boots as soon as possible. With spring came the hope that I would look *cool*, like the Main Street kids who didn't have to wear all the heavy winter clothing that made me waddle like an arthritic penguin.

The April mornings were still cold, however, so my mother still made me suit up when I left for school. One day Spike was just ahead of me on River Street. We didn't walk together—it wasn't cool to walk to school with your brother. When he reached the crest of the hill, I watched as he took off his jacket and gloves and stuffed them into a crevice in the old stone wall.

I stopped. What a great idea! I let him get further ahead and when I got to the wall, I did the same thing. This was great! There were lots of loose rocks and crevices. You could hide all kinds of stuff in there. My hand pulled out a red and white pack of Winstons. Well, that could come in handy for a little blackmail.

When school let out, I walked home, retrieved my clothes from the wall, brushed off the specks of dirt, and put them back on, Mom not any the wiser. At least, not until one day when my clothes disappeared.

There I was, two weeks later, scraping my hands to a bloody pulp as I felt around for the coat and gloves I had left in the crevice that morning. But nothing—not even a button. I was sick. *Maybe she wouldn't notice*, I thought. Sure.

She wasn't in the kitchen when I got home, but the clean scent of Johnson's Wax was, so I knew she was in the house somewhere. Spike sat at the table, pencil in hand, a geography book open in front of him. "Lose something?" he asked. Before I could answer, he continued, "I'll trade you for that pack of Winstons."

Well, there it was. My own brother. Extortion. It wasn't fair—I hadn't gotten a chance to use the cigarettes against *him*.

Uncle John's Funeral

Uncle John, one of my grandfather's brothers, loved a practical joke and there is evidence that he was still pulling them even after he died.

He was one of my favorite great-uncles—always ready for a good laugh. He was also what people called in those days "a bundle of nerves," his body fidgeting and bobbing, constantly in motion. And he was an artist who owned a craft and hobby store.

His wife, Aunt Ginny, on the other hand, was regal and serene—my idea of *cool*. She was a beautician and, I always thought, *glamorous*, the kind of woman who wore bright red lipstick and nail polish, and tortoise-shell combs in her hair. Even when she was working in her garden at Indian Pond, on her knees in the dirt between the stalks of red gladiolas, she wore sundresses with bold, bright flowers, big straw hats, and yellow cotton gloves, her eyes behind sunglasses shaped like cats' eyes with rhinestone frames.

She and Uncle John were artists who painted and carved the things they saw through the big picture window of their camp overlooking the lake: brown mallards, scarlet maple trees, and deep green pines.

Growing Up Cold

They had never had children, which was probably why they loved their nieces and nephews so much—and there were a bunch of us. We spent much of our summers at their camp at Indian Pond. It was called a camp, as in *go up to camp*, but it was nicer than that—a summer home because they spent their winters in Florida. The camp, covered in brown cedar shingles, was tucked away on the edge of the lake in a stand of balsam and cedar so dense that it was almost invisible from the edge of the unpaved road that swung out of the woods and curved to their door, a door which was always open.

If there's a heaven, it is like Uncle John's camp: knotty pine paneling, great fieldstone fireplace, an old upright piano, the aroma of cedar trees and wood smoke, and a candy dish—heaped with toasted-coconut marshmallows. The candy dish sat irresistibly on the coffee table that Uncle John had built from a slab of pine, which still seeped sticky pine pitch on warm days.

There was indoor plumbing but if you felt adventurous, you could use the outhouse that listed under the cover of pine trees behind the boathouse. One summer day, Uncle Joe and couple of his youngest boys were in there changing into their bathing suits and the darn thing fell over with them in it, a story that still comes up at family gatherings to this day.

To get a drink of water, icy cold from the well, you had to prime the hand pump at the blue speckled cast iron sink in the kitchen.

But getting back to Uncle John—he would have had a great time at his funeral, the biggest one in the family since my grandfather had passed away in 1959. People crowded together on the wide porch at Boite's Funeral Home, smoked cigarettes, and told stories about Uncle John's sense of humor and practical jokes. Finally, at the end of the service at Notre Dame, Bobby Boite herded us into our cars and we prepared to follow the hearse to the cemetery across town, all the cars now sporting small black "Funeral" flags on the radio antennas. All, that is, but my cousin Marianne's car: she intended to take her four small children home instead of to the cemetery. She followed the hearse bearing Uncle John's remains out of the church parking lot

63

until it continued straight ahead and disappeared over the crest of Maple Street, then turned her station wagon to the right and headed for home, down Main Street—with the rest of the funeral procession following behind, the hearse by now having disappeared over the hill.

Marianne's home was in the same general direction as the cemetery, so no one realized what exactly had happened until she pulled into her driveway. Glancing back, over a back seat full of children, she finally noticed all the cars. The procession halted, "Funeral" flags fluttering in the summer breeze, as she began pulling babies out of her car and everyone realized what had happened: Uncle John's last practical joke.

Dad's Home Remedies

Some of my father's home remedies.
(Use at your own risk, though they worked for us!)

•   To pull out slivers, my father swore by a black salve that he obtained in small metal tins from the employee nurse at the shop. After a few hours, the salve would force the slivers to work their way up out of the flesh. Called Ichthammol ointment, it is still available in some pharmacies today. The Vermont Country Store in Weston, Vermont, also sells a reasonable facsimile in the form of Petro-Carbo Salve. You can buy it from their catalogues or website.

•   My father told of the time his father saved a favorite horse from the glue factory by soaking her hoof, which was lacerated and had become infected, in a pail of water and the disinfectant Creolin. My father used it to soak our wounds, one teaspoon to a quart of warm water, and I used it myself many years later to cure an infected hangnail.

•   To prevent infection of cuts, pour heated milk over a slice of bread to soak the injured area.

•   Baking soda will cure everything from canker sores to aching feet. For canker sores, make a paste and apply. For sore feet, soak in a solution of baking soda and water.

•   A half teaspoon of baking soda in a cup of warm water will cure indigestion. You'll either burp or "toss" whatever is causing the discomfort.

APRIL

Easter in St. Froid—1958

Dan Sweeney was the DJ on WSTF, St. Froid's own radio station. He was also the news anchor—actually, he was more than just the anchor—he was the whole ship: weatherman, news reporter, announcer, and voice for the commercials that exhorted us to shop at Harvey's Department Store. You could always tell his favorite song, it got a lot of airplay. That year it was Bobby Darin's "Beyond the Sea," also a favorite of mine because my father sang it in French—*La Mer*—while he puttered around the house.

Nineteen fifty-eight was the year that we bought the baby chicks at Woolworth's. We thought it best not to tell Mom and Dad; they had already warned us not to bring any more animals into the house, particularly at this time of the year when we were still waiting for spring and the house seemed a whole lot smaller than it had last October.

Plus, we had never had good luck with pets. They all died. The two bunnies we had when I was two. The three kittens my father brought home to celebrate the birth of my youngest brother, Ricky, when I was four. My turtle, Little Joe, had died of some sort of soft-shell disease. And of our two cats, twin yellow tabbies, one had been hit by a car; the other had a cauliflower ear. You wouldn't have wanted to be a pet in our house. We never seemed to have any pets to enter in the Pet Parade by the time May rolled around. The Pet Parade, an annual event where people would dress up their pets and march them through town in wagons or on bicycles on a Saturday in May, sometimes had over 300 entries. But they were never any of *ours*.

But the chicks pictured in Woolworth's half-page ad in the *St. Froid Times* were just so cute—how could anyone resist them? And only twenty cents apiece! Or you could buy a duckling for the same price.

Woolworth's felt like coming home, especially after fighting a cold headwind all the way across the overpass. The store had its own distinctive smell, a pleasant blend of waxed hardwood floors, Coty face powder, and French fries from the lunch counter. It was the Wal-Mart of the fifties—you could get just about anything you needed there and at a good price. Glass-sided bins and wooden shelves held crocheted potholders, monogrammed handkerchiefs, wooden clothespins, pincushions shaped like tomatoes, oil cans, skeins of wool, baby bibs, and Libby drinking glasses.

As for the chicks, there must have been hundreds of them in the bin: pink, green, and yellow, scrambling around and crawling over each other. They looked frightened and badly in need of rescue. Finally, we settled on a pink chick for me and a yellow one for Ricky. Spike picked out a blue duckling. By noon we were hiking back across the overpass with three squirming paper sacks. I carried a small bag of food pellets.

We decided to keep them in the shed out back. My father seldom went in there—he planned to tear it down the following summer. The shed smelled like dirt and old newspapers—because that's what was in there: dirt floor and boxes of old newspapers, which had come with the house when we bought it. We shredded some of the newspaper and made a nest in a wooden cabinet that was lying on its back. When we went back in the house we left the top of the cabinet ajar so they could breathe.

My mother took me shopping for Easter clothes that afternoon. I really didn't feel like going. You can't work up a lot of enthusiasm for white bonnets and black patent-leather shoes when you have to slog through dirty snow along the sidewalk to get into the store. Plus, I hated shopping for clothes. Although I stood on the threshold of puberty, the door wouldn't open. I was still built like a root beer barrel.

But thanks to my mother's cheerful persistence, the right things magically appeared in the department store and we came home late that afternoon with a bulging green-and-white-striped Harvey's Shoppe bag. My father, an eternal optimist who, despite the snow in the backyard, believed that spring truly was just around the corner, was in the kitchen cleaning out the kerosene stove to put it away for the summer. We showed him my Easter clothes: a white hat with yellow daisies and an elastic strap that creased my jaw and made my face look thinner; black patent-leather shoes that gleamed like licorice; lace-trimmed cuffed white socks; white cotton gloves with darts down the back; and *la piece de resistance*, a yellow—*not* navy blue—coat. It was an *A-line* style, great camouflage for less-than-perfect figures, and made of a new spongy fabric called "bonded acrylic," a fabric so dense that the coat could have gone to church without me.

Easter Morn

We managed to keep the barnyard menagerie a secret for a couple of weeks until one Saturday afternoon when my father went to the shed with a crowbar to start the demolition, and he found our little zoo. He was not happy about it at first, even when we pointed out that they weren't really pets but more like farm animals.

After he calmed down, he said we could keep them until spring when the weather would permit us to navigate the muddy road to Uncle Steve's farm and give them to him. That worked; we spent a lot of time at the farm in the summer so they would still be ours, in a way.

I woke early on Easter morning to a rare brilliant light filtering through the green paper shade on my bedroom window. Could it be—the *sun*? Was spring here at last? Tearing aside the shade, I looked out the window and saw on this April day that the brilliance came from a foot of white, fluffy snow, and it was still coming down like the *Perry Como Christmas Special*. So much for daisies and black patent-leather shoes.

I went downstairs to a kitchen as busy as Brouchette's Diner: Dad shredding cabbage for his killer coleslaw; Mom peeling potatoes that would be ready to cook after we came home from mass. The ham was in the oven, the smoky sweet aroma already warming the room as it started to bake. Cans of Dole pineapple slices and jars of green olives and sweet mixed pickles were lined up like soldiers on the kitchen counter. Grampy, Grammy, and Aunt Aileen were coming for Easter dinner.

"What's wrong?" asked my mother at the look on my face.

"It's snowing," I announced, like this was a big surprise.

But my mother and I wore our Easter outfits anyway, and my father drove right up to the front of the church and let us get out before he went and parked the car, so I wouldn't ruin my new shoes. And inside, the church looked like a garden, packed with Easter bonnets, pink and yellow coats, and white gloves. It takes more than a foot of snow to discourage a Vermonter.

And so it was, another jingle-bell Easter in St. Froid.

"Fou comme un balai."

Old French saying: "Crazy as a broom."

The Rites of Spring

It is impossible to believe, standing in a snowdrift in mid-January, that spring will ever come to the Northeast Kingdom. But one day you're shoveling another snowstorm from the backyard; the next, it seems, you're plucking yellow dandelions from the lawn as melting snow sends a foaming wall of water plowing down the Oompassaic River.

Springtime is rhubarb time. Rhubarb is a bitter vegetable, but in Vermont, after a long gray winter, people tend to grab any green shoot, no matter how unpalatable, and cook it. Rhubarb. Dandelion greens. Once when I was four, I pulled a fistful of tiger lily shoots out of the ground and ate them, thinking they were string beans. I've forgotten what they tasted like but they couldn't have been any worse than unsweetened rhubarb. But give my mother some rhubarb and a pound or two of sugar and she would bake the most delicious, sweet-tart rhubarb pie you have ever eaten.

Leave it to Vermonters to take this time of year, which combines the dreariness of winter and the cheerless experience of mud season, and make a game out of it. The people of the village of Indian Pond have a contest that has proven to be a more accurate predictor of spring than that rodent in Pennsylvania. They hold a year-long lottery as to what date and time the ice on the pond will melt. Anyone can pay a dollar to submit a guess at the Indian Pond General Store— the money eventually divided between the winner of the lottery and the Indian Pond Association, which maintains the beach, boating access areas, and provides the annual Fourth of July fireworks over the pond. Tourists who stop their cars next to the wide wooden porch and step into the general store for postcards and maple syrup are intrigued, and will take a moment to jot down their guesses and drop them into a mason jar on the counter, next to the home-baked bread and brownies heaped by the cash register. Cleon Smith, the owner of the store as well as the postmaster of the village of Indian Pond, lives on the lake year round and is in charge of determining when the exact time occurs. He ties a cord to a cinder block and puts it on a wooden pallet on the frozen lake behind his cottage. Then he ties the other end to an electric clock on the back porch. When the ice melts, the cinder block plunges into the lake or floats away on the wood; either way, the clock is unplugged. As long as they've been keeping records, the earliest that the ice has melted was on April 18, the latest on May 6.

The actual first sign of spring, when I was a kid, was when our mothers finally let us take off some of our woolies for the walk to school. We were suddenly weightless, like that trick, you know, where you push your arms real hard up against a doorframe and when you step out your arms just float up on their own? What a relief after carrying around all that extra padding since November. What a relief to leave it all in the closet. Ski pants, parkas, boots, scarves, earmuffs, gloves. Our eyes, no longer shaded by hoods and scarves, squinted in the unaccustomed brightness of the new spring sun, and for the first time since Thanksgiving, we could see and hear where we were going.

I, personally, was anxious to strip off the ugly cotton-knit tights— supposedly flesh-colored but only in the way that an ace bandage is flesh-colored—which my mother insisted I wear to keep my legs warm under my uniform.

And so, as the air grew warmer, it brought with it a renewed hope that, *this* year, finally, I would be *cool*.

"Ca me fend le cul."

Old French saying of indignation:
"Well, *that* really splits my butt!"

MAY

The Saga of Sister Saint Cecilia's Clicker

May was a heady time of year in St. Froid. Like a dull young girl who at last reaches a wild and untamed puberty, springtime exploded on our black-and-white Vermont world in daffodil yellow and lilac blue. It was spring. Anything was possible.

For us Catholics, May was the month of Mary. That year, 1960, a blonde-haired seventh grader, Muguette DuBois, had crowned the statue of our Lady during a procession on the first Sunday of May, as the congregation sang "C'est le mois de Marie, c'est le mois le plus beau." *It's the month of Mary, the most beautiful month.* And May was time for First Communion.

There was tension that time of year among the sixth grade girls at Mount St. Helene's as we wondered who among us would the teachers choose to be the angels for First Communion who lead the children in the procession. It was a great honor to be an angel for First Communion—the Catholic equivalent of Miss Dairy Queen. But being chosen the Lead Angel was even bigger. The Lead Angel got to use Sister Saint Cecilia's wooden clicker: two small pieces of wood, hinged together, that she used whenever she had to herd us together, marching from the convent to mass, letting us know when to stop or go, stand or sit.

The idea was that the Lead Angel would signal to the children all the appropriate times to kneel, stand or sit at mass, so that they would all do it in unison. This was something taken quite seriously at Mount St. Helene's: to walk in single file and to do everything in unison.

That year the nuns chose Katy, Patsy, and me to be the angels. And to the wonder of all, they chose me to be the Lead Angel.

You can well imagine the surprise. No one could believe it...*Lucille*...who Sister Mary Margaret said would never amount to a hill of beans because she couldn't shut up in class. *Lucille*...who had shattered convent records that had stood for more than one hundred years for the most broken windows, intercepted notes, and sprained ankles.

I was surprised myself. But then again, studies show that the oldest child in a family is a natural leader.

The angel costume was really cool, wings and all. The long, flowing gown was cinched at the waist with a white silk cord. It looked good on Patsy, slender as she was; Katy and I looked like a couple of deranged lampshades.

As for the wings, Spike and Ricky thought I could really fly with them. They dared me to jump off the roof of Red Voisin's garage. Spike had already tried that, sort of, the summer before. He'd been playing on the roof and first thing he knew he was rolling off. Although he fell about 15 feet he didn't break anything, but something had happened to his head: he couldn't remember how he had gotten home, or even his own name, for several hours after it happened. His guardian angel must have been with him, is all I can say. But then, Spike's guardian angel had very little time off.

The outfit was crowned with a circle of daisies, perched on the fluffy pouf of my brand new Toni perm.

First Communion Day finally arrived and the weather was perfect—blue sky and cotton-ball clouds—we didn't even need our coats. It was the kind of spring morning that almost makes up for those long Vermont winters.

As for me, I wasn't nervous at all. I had been practicing for weeks and besides, how many times had I been to mass in my life already? I could negotiate the order of the mass as well as I could the curves on River Road. Piece of cake.

And so we began. A line of children dressed like brides and grooms, quieter than they had ever been, followed me solemnly down the red-carpeted center aisle of Notre Dame. The organ played to a full house while Katy and Patsy each led their group down the side aisles. I stopped at the front pews, marked with black velvet "Reserved" signs and, with one click, directed the children to file into the pews, one by one.

Finally, all were where they belonged and Father LaSalle began the mass.

Everything went smoothly until we got to the Consecration, the part of the mass where everyone kneels. I was distracted by Bobby DuBois, one of the boys from St. Bernard's School, so I totally missed my cue. When I finally realized where we were in the service, the children and congregation had already, without benefit of my clicker, gone to their knees. But I didn't notice that either. Firmly and with great authority, I clicked the clicker. After all that rehearsing, the children, reacting in predictable Pavlovian response, rose to their feet in one great wave. Hearing the commotion, and following the children's lead, the entire congregation also rose to its feet.

Oh, shit! My suddenly slippery palms began clicking furiously like a hysterical flamenco dancer, as people popped up and down and tried to obey the signals, some of them looking dizzy by now. *If they ever kneel again*, I thought, *I'll stop clicking and leave them there*. But the trick was to catch them on the way down. Finally! They were kneeling again. I closed the clicker gently, then gratefully knelt myself. Hearing the commotion, Father LaSalle looked up from the altar, his eyes saying *enough!* I didn't dare look at Sister Saint Cecilia. We sang "Come Holy Gho-o-o-st, Creator blest…"

After the ceremony, Sister slid the clicker out of my hand and deep into the folds of her black habit. She was reluctant to give up custody of her clicker after that. But it didn't matter because soon the tradition of angels for First Communion went the way of the Latin mass, girls wearing hats in church, and fish on Friday.

But I don't think all of that was *my* fault.

It's not the long, cold winters that can
make a Vermonter mean;
it's those short, cold summers.

— Chris Maistros, 1989

JUNE

Summer Rituals: Hair

On a Saturday morning in mid-June, Dad would take the boys for their annual summer buzz cuts. Later, you could smell the Bay Rum hair tonic while they were still in the driveway. Stunned—like new recruits at Fort Dix—they stood for a while in the kitchen, brushing their stubby fingers across their bristly little heads, their wintry pink scalps showing through. Looking back, this was eerily portentous of the way the boys in our neighborhood would look ten years later, at the height of the Vietnam War.

But that was later. This was the fifties, an era not memorable for great hairstyles. I can't imagine future generations recalling wistfully the Mamie Eisenhower look that my mother wore back then: flat on top with a center part, pin-curled sides, and bangs turned under, as if they'd been wound around a sausage. Some women actually went shopping in pin curls and babushkas.

My own hair was naturally straight. It was, that is, until the mid-sixties when straight hair came into style and my hair then perversely decided to become wavy.

I usually wore the Korean refugee look: combed straight down from a center part to a fringe that just brushed the top of my ears, the bangs cut blunt and straight across my forehead.

Sometimes my friend Patsy's mom would give her a Toni, and for a while Patsy looked like Little Orphan Annie, except she had eyes. Some of the older boys in the neighborhood, like "Deuce" Clouatre and "Red" Voisin, wore DAs, the hair on the back of their heads Bryl-Creamed into a slick, feathery resemblance of a duck's rear end.

My father was the only person I knew who never bowed to fashion. His dark wavy hair was styled the same in all the photos I have ever seen of him, from the time he was a small boy until he died at age 75: not too short on the top and parted on the side.

I believe that the long, bushy-hair thing of the late sixties was inevitable, a direct result of the hairstyles of the fifties. I remember a Polaroid shot of my brothers and their girlfriends standing with their arms around each other on my father's lawn in the summer of 1969 and, between the beards and long hair, you can't tell where one person starts and the other leaves off.

The Yankee Law of Natural Retribution

Law #2: If you sing at the dinner table,
you'll cry before bedtime

More on a Hairy Topic

Hair—the kind you have or the style you wear—is very important in trying to achieve *cool*ness. My hair never looked quite right. When everyone began wearing it long and straight, like Mary who sang with Peter and Paul, mine grew so thick that it wouldn't lie flat. I was obsessed with it. Nothing I did could reduce what I perceived to be a hump on the top of my head.

One day after school, in a fit of desperation, I took my mother's sewing shears, grabbed a fistful of the top layer and cut it off about three inches from the top of my head. It was the first time I had ever heard my mother shriek. I explained to her that it had just been too thick to do anything with. "It's thinner now, all right," she agreed. I should have left it alone. When Aunt Ginny saw it, she said the only choice was to cut it short, in layers, or live with a chunk of hair, about six inches shorter than the rest and right in the middle of the back of my head. It just wasn't fair.

My hair also felt really dry, sometimes, and flyaway. I read in a magazine to use olive oil: work the olive oil into the scalp, cover it with plastic wrap and let it marinate for a few hours. Then wash it out.

We were not olive oil people. Italians used olive oil. We used butter, oleo, and Crisco. The only thing I could think of that might be a good substitute was Vaseline.

I worked a good glob of Vaseline into my scalp and into the hair, from the roots to the ends. Then I wrapped my head in plastic wrap and lay down on my bed to read. I fell asleep. By late afternoon, I had been lying there about four hours. Time to wash the treatment out of my hair.

The first couple of soapings with Prell shampoo made not one bit of difference—my hair was still as slick as an otter's. This was going to take some work. My father glanced up from Saturday's *St. Froid Times* as I passed through the kitchen with the Joy dishwashing liquid and went back into the bathroom. Several soapings later, my fingers were wrinkled but the gummy residue still glued my hair to my head. I looked like a flapper—all I needed were the Betty Boop spit curls near my ears. Then Dad called me for supper.

Forced to leave the cover of the bathroom, I went to the supper table. When I sat down, my father raised his head, and then his eyebrows.

"I thought you were going to wash your hair," he asked.

"I did! Can't you *tell?*" So, maybe I was a little defensive. In tears, I told him what I had done. He and my mother looked at me in disbelief.

"Vaseline? In your hair?"

Trying not to laugh, my siblings choked down their hot dogs while my parents studied me like a specimen in a petrie dish. My father suggested a few more hits of Joy and a vinegar rinse.

By morning, I was surprised to find a sizeable grease mark on my pillow—since my head kept sliding off all night long, I never imagined it was on the pillow long enough to leave a mark. The next day at mass, the hat I had pulled down almost to my ears slid upward slowly, through the whole service, and threatened to pop off and expose my head to the entire congregation. I shampooed it a few more times on Sunday afternoon and by the time I left for school on Monday morning you could hardly tell what I had done. Except, somehow, my hair looked dry and greasy at the same time.

Other Summer Rituals: Lifesaving

We could live with bad haircuts. There was something else that ruined our summers: swimming lessons. We'd sooner have volunteered to muck out the cow stalls at Uncle Steve's farm.

My father reacted to our moans, as he usually did, with a story. "You've got to learn how to swim," he told us. "Didn't you know I saved somebody's life one time, because I could swim?"

We were astonished. He went on to tell us about his friend who went "down for the third time," and when you go down for the third time, your whole life passes before you, like in a movie, and then you drown.

They were swimming in the river that cut through my grandfather's farm when this friend, Joe Francis, developed a cramp or something and started to drown. Dad swam right over to him, grabbed him under the arms and pulled him to the riverbank. "You might get to meet him, one of these days," Dad told us, "when we go to Canada—he works at the Customs House in Highwater."

Highwater? This guy who almost drowned now worked in a place called *Highwater?*

Sure enough, the next time we went to visit our cousins in Canada, Mr. Francis was on duty at the Canadian Customs station. As my father climbed out of the car, Mr. Francis, a tall man in a black uniform, graying hair and glasses, rushed over to shake his hand. We stayed in the back seat but I rolled down the window to get a closer look at him, the man whose life my father had saved. It was hard to imagine that he had once been a boy, struggling for his life. Wow. You just never knew.

"So that's why you *have* to take swimming lessons," my father finished, "because you never know."

I really *did* want to learn how to swim but it wasn't worth what we had to endure. Despite three or four wasted summers of my girlhood, I could barely do the dog paddle. First, I was uncomfortable parading around in front of people in a bathing suit. It didn't help that the fashion at the time was ruffles, lots of them that flounced around on my butt like a beach umbrella in a stiff wind. Why couldn't I look like Susie, the lifeguard and our swimming instructor, who wore a sophisticated black bathing suit and whose slender brown legs were long enough to brush the concrete when she sat high up in the lifeguard chair?

Then there was the mile-and-a-half trek across town just to get to the pool, our bathing suits rolled up in a towel. Even on a cool summer morning, my t-shirt would be soaked with sweat by the time I got there. This was good: I would soon need all the heat I could generate.

Which brings me to the third and most important reason to dread swimming lessons: we were always assigned to the first class of the morning: 9:30 a.m. And because it was daylight savings time, it was actually 8:30 a.m. And *nobody* goes swimming in Vermont in June at 8:30 in the morning.

So I would go and I would splash around for the first couple of lessons, and then, one morning in July, I'd tell my mother I didn't feel good. "Don't listen to yourself," she'd say, "you might feel better after you get moving."

But she'd check my forehead, just in case, because of what had happened at Indian Pond in the summer of 1958. It was early June and unseasonably warm in St. Froid, the thermometer at the People's Bank on Depot Street registering a sweltering 72 degrees at high noon. The boys and I had persuaded my kind but reluctant maiden aunt, Aileen, to take us swimming. When we got to the lake, ten miles away at the top of the first mountain west of town where a steady wind blows year round, the wind chill was about 50 degrees. So, we cancelled our swim, bundled up in sweaters and, instead, went for a boat ride. Aunt Aileen was at the oars when I reached over the side to trail my hand in the cold, black water and fell overboard. She called my name as I disappeared over the side of the wooden boat, Aunt Ginny's old gray sweater and all. If my life passed before me that day, it was too short to remember. I developed pneumonia and subsequently spent ten days in the hospital. Contrary to what grown-ups had always told us, the pneumonia didn't kill me, plus I actually lost eleven pounds, so it wasn't all bad. But it had made my mother extremely nervous whenever I sneezed.

Back to the swimming lessons. In the women's locker room, I changed into my bathing suit. Even today, the potpourri of damp towels, wet sneakers, and chlorine tightens my chest with anxiety. Then I walked barefoot to poolside, gingerly trying to avoid the icky puddles containing God knows how many germs, to join the line of shivering, blue-lipped children huddled together at the edge of the pool, like victims of a firing squad. We stood there, thighs speckled with goosebumps, the girls in colorful bathing caps like a row of beach balls, while the instructor tried to get us to ditch our towels and jump into the water.

This went on for three or four summers until my mother, tired of listening to our whining, stopped making us go. As a result, Ricky learned to hate the water, and never goes near it. Spike did learn the sidestroke, and I mastered the dogpaddle, but not well enough so that the lifeguards let me jump off the high diving board. In order to be permitted to do that, swimmers had to demonstrate that they could swim two laps across the widest part of the pool. I tried, once, but in the middle of the second lap, the lifeguard noticed my obvious distress and tossed me a life preserver. I almost turned it down because he was really cute and I thought I'd rather drown than suffer the humiliation. After that incident, the word got around in the lifeguard locker room and they would never let me try it again.

As far as I know, there are no Olympic swimmers from Vermont.

"*C'est pas luis qui a invente les pattes de mouche.*"
"He's not the one who invented flies' feet."

Old French saying akin to "He's not too bright."

The Dump

There were rats at the dump, but we had never actually seen any. Hunters in plaid jackets and wool caps came to the dump to practice their skills shooting at them, but we liked to go to the dump with my father because it was an adventure.

This should not reflect on my parents or our lifestyle. Going to the dump was a weekly ritual for many people in St. Froid back then.

We begged my father to go with him when, on a Saturday morning, he announced that today was the day to take the rubbish—which is differentiated from "garbage" in that it isn't juicy. Rubbish is cardboard boxes and torn sofa cushions; garbage is banana peels and coffee grounds. We'd hurry and dress in dungarees and t-shirts while Dad would open the cellar door and begin to haul out boxes of trash. There were no large plastic trash bags in those days, which made the hauling a lot more work. On the other hand, the town allowed people to burn rubbish and yard waste in discarded oil drums in their back yards, which saved a lot of hauling, so I guess it all balanced out.

When he finished loading the car, sometimes having to tie the trunk down because it wouldn't close, we jumped into the car and he would drive away. The dump was actually right in town, on a hill behind Saxon's Wagon and Tool Works. We could tell we were almost there by the smell; there was always something self-combusting and smoldering in the mountains of rubbish. The smell was not altogether unpleasant, though, which was good because sometimes you could get a whiff of it downtown.

A man worked there, guarding the dump, I guess. He had a small shack by the entrance, a sentry's booth, like the ones the Beefeaters stand in at Buckingham Palace, but not as grand.

What made the dump so exciting, besides the possibility of seeing a rat, was what other people had thrown out. The dump was like a trading post. Although we weren't allowed to touch anything, we could window shop. Items left near the "sentry's" booth, not dumped on the refuse heaps, were still clean and useable. One person would drop off a carton of *Life* magazines from the back of a station wagon, browse the other boxes, and maybe pick up a case of *Look*. Someone else would come along and leave encyclopedias or *Reader's Digest Condensed Books* in brown paper sacks. An antique junkie would go crazy if he or she could go back to that time and place to sort through the crocks and clocks, cast-iron frying pans and St. Froid Farms milk bottles, paint-by-number oil paintings, piano stools and books, books, books.

Maybe that's when my love of rooting through the back rooms of antique shops was born.

JULY

The Silver Moon Summer of 1955

The only thing that was fashionable about the early fifties was the American car. Cars had personality back then: there was no confusing a 1948 Desoto with a 1955 Ford.

I knew quite a bit about the 1948 DeSoto because in 1955, the summer after our return from California (see October), my father traded his truck for one. Although I was only seven that summer when everyone was singing "The Ballad of Davy Crockett," I remember a lot about that car—maybe because it was a memorable summer for more than one reason.

We were living in the front half of Uncle Joe's duplex on Spring Street, a neighborhood that typified the postwar explosion of children; between Uncle Joe's family and ours there were nine kids living in this house alone. My mother was in the kitchen and we were watching the Mickey Mouse Club one afternoon when my father got home from the shop, climbed the steps to the front porch, and called to us through the screen door that he had a surprise. There, parked at the curb, was a huge four-door DeSoto Custom Suburban, with white sidewall tires and suicide doors. It was olive green with real wood-grain trim inside and a radio. We wanted to go for a ride right then, but my father had other plans: after supper, he was taking us to the Silver Moon Drive-In Theater.

"You never heard of the Silver Moon Drive-In Theater?" he asked, feigning astonishment. He loved to introduce us to new things. The Silver Moon Drive-In Theater, he said, was *outdoor* movies. You could sit in your car and watch the movie through the windshield. *Well!*

I had been to the movies once, the indoor movies, with my cousin, Missy. After Dad had dropped us in front of St. Froid's two movie theaters, the Star and the Palace, for the Saturday afternoon matinee, we had gone into the wrong one and seen a love story rather than the Disney film we were supposed to see. The mistake was understandable. Neither Missy nor I could read very well. Today, the movie would probably have been rated PG-13; nevertheless, Dad and Uncle Joe were not happy when they came to pick us up in Uncle Joe's Jeep at 4:30 that afternoon. Pulling up in front of the theaters, they parked the Jeep and scanned the mob of kids milling around in front of the Palace, and then watched as, two small heads bobbing in a sea of adults, we sauntered out of the Star. I hadn't been back to the movies since.

After supper, we got back in the DeSoto and left for the movies. Now that we had a car instead of a truck, there was room for the whole family to ride together. *Heck*, all five of us could have ridden in the front, it was so big, and left room for Uncle Joe's family in the back. And there were many more windows than there had been in the truck. I, being the oldest, got a window seat, and Spike took the other one. Ricky was actually better off in the middle when the car bounced over the ruts at the entrance to the drive-in and a gray cloud of dust billowed out from under the white sidewalls and into the open windows.

A giant wood fence, like the one in *King Kong*, surrounded the theater so people couldn't sneak in or watch the movie from the side of Route 5. My father paid the man at the gate and then drove from one row of parking spots to another, each row a wave of dirt, cresting and ebbing like the surf at Old Orchard Beach. Finally, he parked, leaned out the window and pulled in the speaker, a gray box with a button on the front like a radio, and hung it on the driver's side window. Then he rolled up the window about halfway to hold it in place.

As we kids sat in the backseat, too awed by the experience to fight with each other, Dad asked, "Does anyone want some popcorn?"

Did I want popcorn? I was a popcorn junkie. To me snacking was an activity. I liked something that lasted awhile, so I ate popcorn very slowly, one buttery kernel at a time. If I had my way, there would be popcorn in heaven, barrels of it, next to the vats of ginger ale.

Then my father asked me if *I* wanted to go get it. It was the first time he had given me any responsibility that involved money. I was thrilled. He handed me a dollar and told me to get some pop, too. I slid off the back seat and hurried down the dusty path to the snack bar before he could change his mind.

The man behind the counter in a white button-down shirt and black slacks asked me what I wanted. I ordered five popcorns and five root beers. And when he asked *Small, Medium, Large or Jumbo*, it slipped out before I could stop it: "*Jumbo.*"

As soon as the word was out of my mouth, I thought of my brothers. Spike, five years old—his supper usually ended up wreathing the tablecloth under the rim of his plate. Ricky, three—his diet consisted mainly of peanut butter and Cheerios. Not only had I ordered *Jumbo* popcorns, but *Jumbo* soda—I looked around to see if this place had a toilet. My mouth went dry but it was too late to change the order—the man had lined it all up on the counter above my head. "That'll be two bucks," he said, waiting. *Two* dollars? Uh oh. "I'll be right back," I told him.

I thought of running away from home, darting through the rows of cars until I found some nice, elderly couple, like Uncle John and Aunt Ginny, who didn't have any kids and maybe would let me live with them. But I hadn't even seen the movie yet. I went back to the car to ask my father for another dollar.

"Another *dollar?*" he said, as if I had asked him for enough money to buy the theater. "Oh, my aching back—" For my father, this statement was just one degree below cursing, a warning that he was very upset.

"How could you spend two whole dollars on just popcorn and soda?"

He found out when he took me back to the snack bar and saw all that stuff lined up on the counter.

It was a long time before Dad gave me that kind of responsibility again, but like all junkies, my humiliation did not overcome my lust for popcorn.

Polecat

I was a clumsy child with weak ankles, ungraceful and always falling down. I spent most of my childhood limping.

I was a heckuva climber, though.

On a Saturday afternoon, a week or two after what I would always think of as the "Silver Moon Popcorn Disaster," I decided to climb the Central Vermont Public Service utility pole by the porch in front of our house. It was almost suppertime and I had the front porch all to myself. Climbing poles wasn't near as challenging as climbing trees; there were iron rungs running up the sides of them. Dad had warned us to stay away from these poles, that the wires could electrocute you, but I didn't plan to climb high enough to touch a wire. I tried to ignore the impulse, which made it predictably more alluring. I soon found myself at the base of the pole, reaching up to grab one of the iron spikes. I found a toehold with my sneakers and started up. The spikes were farther apart than they appeared from the ground, but all that tree climbing was paying off. I was about nine feet off the ground when the car came down the street.

I stopped and looked down to see the black and white car roll past: the St. Froid Police Department. We watched the new television show *HighwayPatrol*, and I saw myself in handcuffs, tossed into the back seat by a scowling Broderick Crawford.

Lucille Maurice Maistros

I hugged the pole and tried not to move as the cruiser slowed and came to a stop right under my feet.

A voice called, "So what're you up to?" I prepared to climb down. "Oh, not much. How 'bout *you*?"

It was old man Scott, our neighbor across the street, standing behind his lawnmower in a cloud of my favorite summer scent: fresh-cut grass and gasoline vapors.

They hadn't seen me! Yet.

They talked and talked as I clung like a squirrel to the side of the pole. After what seemed like weeks, the cruiser rolled off down the street and turned the corner, out of sight onto Main Street.

It took me a lot less time to come down than it had to go up. For a few minutes, I hid behind the porch railing in case they came back. Then Mr. Scott, who had never even seemed to look up from the mower, put in his two cents. "You shouldn't do that, you know, it's dangerous. You could get electrocuted." At least he hadn't ratted on me.

I had gotten away with it, without killing myself or even getting a sliver. Well—what do you know.

God Has a Sense of Humor

When the accident happened, on a Friday, two days before the Fourth of July that summer of 1955, I learned that it doesn't pay to get too cocky.

It was an ordinary kid's swing that got me in the end, something even small children could safely use...as long as they don't stand on the swing...as long as they don't push it as high as possible...and as long as they don't then let go and fall off and break one of their arms. Which is what I did.

"What's wrong now?" my mother asked, when she heard me crying at the screen door.

By the time my father came home, the aspirin had taken effect and I wasn't feeling all that bad, except scared of being in trouble. He wasn't too happy about it. He got his leather belt out of the closet so I'm thinking, *this is it—he's going to wallop me with the belt*, although he had never done that before. But instead he buckled it around the back of my neck and slid my arm through it. He said he would take me to Dr. Foley's clinic in the morning, on Saturday.

The clinic! I hated the clinic. It smelled of things that stung, like mercurochrome and rubbing alcohol, and it seemed like you couldn't get out of there without getting a shot. A shot was about the worst thing that could happen to a kid but it was Dr. Foley's answer to every affliction known to man, woman, or kid. Hangnail? "Give her a shot." Bad haircut? "Give her a shot."

I was five years old the first time I remember going to the clinic. I had tried to push a hankie through the wringer of the washing machine. The wringer was too fast for me, I yanked the hankie and my hand through before my mother knew what was happening. Turning around in time to see my elbow passing through, she hit the emergency release button and the rollers parted. There was pain coupled with a sense of relief that my arm wasn't flat.

Then my mother had loaded us, three-year-old Spike and I, into Spike's red Mercury wagon and hauled us to the clinic, taking the shortcut over the railroad tracks and up the gully to Depot Street. My arm was not broken that time, but sure enough, because of a slight cut, Dr. Foley had given me a tetanus shot.

So, this summer of 1955 when I was seven, while Dr. Foley examined my arm, I prepared myself for the worse.

"She'll need to get an x-ray," he told my father. An x-ray? What the heck was an x-ray, a super-sized shot? I was terrified. "Is it going to hurt?"

But he just stood me behind a frosted glass window, pushed a couple of buttons and took a picture of the bone. Now *that* was cool!

Afterwards Dr. Foley, puffing on a Camel, studied the film and confirmed that my arm was indeed broken about three inches below the shoulder blade. I waited for him to tell me it would have to come off. Or that I would need a shot. But he said it was a nice clean break and that, thanks to my father's sling, it had already started to heal and I wouldn't need a cast. This was good news as my cousin Missy, Uncle Joe's daughter, had told me all about having her leg in a cast after she'd been struck by a car last summer, and how she couldn't take baths or go to the pool or anything.

Dr. Foley put my arm in a fabric sling and pinned it to some cotton bandages he had wrapped around my middle about four times, very tight, so I couldn't move it or try to use it for anything. I could already feel an itch starting on my chest, deep inside the cotton swathing.

Then he told me I'd have to wear it for about six weeks—and I couldn't get it wet.

Six *weeks*? All summer without going to the Kiwanis pool or Indian Pond? But that was the best part of the whole summer, which now stretched bleakly toward September. And *next* summer, well, in kid time, it might as well have been the next century.

I was trying not to cry when we left but Dad said we could go down to Aunt Mary's Vermont Soda Fountain on Depot Street and get a couple of root-beer floats. Aunt Mary, my grandfather's sister, a widow who had lost her young husband to tuberculosis, was a pretty woman with coal black hair piled high on her head. Dad pushed the door open to the aroma of fresh-brewed coffee and the clatter of forks on plates. It was mid-morning and Aunt Mary was wiping the counter when we went in. The soda fountain was long and narrow with stools on one side and booths on the other. On the counter were lemon meringue pies, chocolate layer cakes, and my grandmother's doughnuts heaped on platters under glass lids.

The booths were jammed full but we found two stools at the counter. She brought the pot of coffee right over but Dad said we wanted root-beer floats. "And, by the way, how about some of that chocolate cake?" This was a major treat—we weren't the kind of people who went out to eat much.

When we left Aunt Mary's place, instead of getting into the car, my father took me by my good hand next door to Uncle John's Hobby Shop. Now *that* was a cool place: a craft and toy store that always smelled faintly of hair-permanent solution because Aunt Ginny's beauty parlor was in the back half of the building. There were puzzles and games, model cars and trains and paint-by-number kits, metal machines for making potholders, knitting needles and yarn, Ava Gardner paper dolls, and Roy Rogers's coloring books. I browsed while Dad told them about my arm, Aunt Ginny "tsk, tsking" the whole time.

Then my father said I could choose anything I wanted—anything in the store.

Anything I wanted? Opportunities like this come along only once in a kid's life—even at Christmas, you don't get a chance to browse in a store and choose whatever you want. But there was a lot of pressure, too. I didn't want to blow it by choosing something I would be bored with in a week.

What I chose, maybe because of our visit to Aunt Mary's, was a Betty Crocker Baking Set complete with spatulas, chocolate cake mix, small plastic bowls and cake pans. My yen for the impractical was doing me in this time: how can you stir and bake if you can't use both arms? But after we got home, my father held the bowl steady while I stirred with my left hand.

So breaking my arm wasn't *all* bad, but because I couldn't go to the pool, it was still one of the longest summers of my life. However, for a Vermonter, that's a *good* thing.

"Don't listen to yourself."

My mother's philosophy of not
giving in to illness or adversity.

The First Vermont
Fourth of July

Although French explorer Jacques Cartier was the first European to see what is now Vermont, it was Samuel de Champlain, traveling with a group of friendly Algonquins, who discovered Lake Champlain on July 4, 1609, and became the French godfather, so to speak, of the Green Mountain State. "Mon Dieux!" he most likely said, "it is cold for Juillet! And how's about those black flies!" Or words to that effect.

Later, in 1775, Ethan Allen and the Green Mountain Boys captured Fort Ticonderoga and did their part to help the thirteen original colonies in the War for Independence. Taking independence even one step further, Vermont declared *itself* an independent republic in 1777. Vermont finally became the fourteenth state in 1791. To celebrate the occasion, or maybe just to do a little advance campaigning for the presidency, Thomas Jefferson and James Madison both visited Vermont that same year. Then things were quiet for a while, and for years, it was said that the Green Mountain state had more cows than people.

However, things picked up again when Vermont was rediscovered in the late 1960s by gangs of youth, non-conformist rebels who nevertheless arrived in uniforms of colorful tie-dyed t-shirts and leather peace-sign pendants. They drove their chartreuse Volkswagen buses north from the great cities of Connecticut and New York, gray plumes of aromatic smoke drifting out the open windows. For the most part, they drove leisurely enough to successfully negotiate the hills and curves of U.S. Route 5 and arrived to establish communes and raise goats on the clovered hillsides.

Some of them lasted through only one Vermont winter, but others put down deeper roots. Today they sell their goat cheese and Vermont hardwood products in glossy catalogues and on the Internet.

They still prefer to drive old Route 5, gray ponytails whipping out the windows of their BMWs and Subarus.

Hair and Other Summer Rituals: The Sequel

By July 1961, I was in puberty, full swing. Or maybe I should say, *mood* swing. Spike nicknamed me "crabby." I was thirteen that summer and had spent twenty-five cents on my first 45 record: *Exodus* by Ferrante and Teicher. It wasn't rock and roll but the music of the twin pianos was so moving that I had to own it for myself.

There were signs that my parents had noticed my budding maturity: I was now permitted to stay up later on school nights so I could watch *Ben Casey*, which Dr. Zorba opened with the words "Man...woman...birth...death...infinity." The "man...woman" part sounded somewhat sexy.

I couldn't wait to start shaving my legs. My mother wasn't as anxious. At first, she'd bought me some special sandpaper mitts that you are supposed to rub over your legs to remove the hair. That worked for a while but then the stubble got tougher and it took too long to do the job. By the time June rolled around and I was invited to Marcie Bennett's seventh grade graduation party at her camp at Indian Pond, I had decided to use my father's double-edged razor and his Burma Shave. A couple of boys from church were invited and everyone would be wearing bathing suits. The pressure was on.

116

Growing Up Cold

The Friday afternoon before the party, I locked myself in the bathroom and got to work. I was safe from interruption for two hours or so. Mom and Dad always met at the A&P after work on Fridays, and Spike and Ricky were outdoors playing. I took off my clothes and got into the bathtub so I wouldn't make a mess on the floor. Then I wet my legs and patted on the shaving cream nice and thick and got started.

It looked like the first thing I was going to have to learn was how to stop the bleeding. The second thing, related to the first, was that I didn't have to apply a lot of pressure to the razor.

While I was trying to stop the bleeding with my father's styptic pencil—the only thing more painful would have been to pour rubbing alcohol on grass cuts—I noticed the hair on my arms. And the tops of my thighs. And the tops of my feet. Seized suddenly by the need to be purely and totally free of body hair, I sprayed the shave cream everywhere and started scraping.

By 5 o'clock, Spike was screaming to use the bathroom and I was mopping up the mess. It wouldn't do to have my parents discover me, like an Incan sacrifice, in the bathtub with blood all over the place. They might never let me near a razor again. I would have to work in a carnival sideshow—*Baboon Girl*. Besides, I was finally getting the hang of it and only cut myself three more times.

The next day, Saturday, dawned cool and rainy. We stayed bundled in sweatshirts and dungarees all afternoon, roasting hot dogs and marshmallows in Marcie's fireplace. My body, although patched with a network of Band-Aids, was as shiny and hair-free as a bowling ball but nobody would get to see it. And it would all grow back and I'd have to do it all over again.

This growing up business was starting to look like a lot of trouble.

AUGUST

Freewheeling

A s the summer of 1961 drifted along, I was spending more of my allowance on records: *Hello, Mary Lou* by Ricky Nelson. *Running Scared* by Roy Orbison. Mom and Dad liked Lawrence Welk's *Calcutta*.

I was now allowed to stay up past ten o'clock on Saturday nights. After we had all had our baths, we watched Giselle McKenzie, Snooky Lansom, and Dorothy Collins on *Your Hit Parade*, then *The Honeymooners* on *The Jackie Gleason Show*, followed by Richard Boone in *Have Gun – Will Travel*. Then the boys and Cissy went to bed at ten o'clock while I took another hit or two of ginger ale and watched Marshall Dillon and Miss Kitty in *Gunsmoke*. I had a crush on the new guy, Quint Asper, the blacksmith, the first time I remember seeing Burt Reynolds.

We had had some terrific thunderstorms that summer. My mother, an otherwise courageous woman, was terrified of lightning. Whenever Dan Sweeney on WSTF predicted anything more than a light sprinkle, she would pull the wooden crucifix from her bedroom wall, the one every Catholic family owned for the priest to use to give Extreme Unction when someone was very sick or dying. The crucifix was hollow, and inside were two beeswax candles, cotton balls and holy oil. She would place the candles in the brass holders, one at the end of each arm of the crucifix, and light them. And we would huddle together in her bedroom until the storm passed.

I spent much of that summer riding my bike, a hand-me-down Columbia from the Dubee twins who went to our church, blue with white sidewall tires. It had a metal basket attached to the handlebars and a flat passenger seat on the rim over the rear tire.

I really loved that bike, that is, until Roxanna Genovese got a shiny new, black English bike with hand controls and skinny tires. Very modern. Very *cool*. My old trusty bike now felt like a mule.

For weeks, I had begged her to let me ride it, but she was reluctant. "It was really expensive," she said, "my parents would kill me."

By the end of August, though, I had pretty much worn down her resolve. As bored by then as I was, she finally agreed to let me ride it if I promised that I wouldn't go far, just down Mountain Avenue. She showed me how to shift the gears and how to stop the bike with the handbrakes. Yes! I could not believe I was really going to get to do this.

I made a u-turn in our driveway and started toward the street. As I rolled down Mountain Avenue, air whistling past my ears, the intersection of River Street rushed up toward me like a film in fast-forward. Trying to slow down, I pushed the pedals in reverse: nothing happened.

No brakes! What happened to the brakes?! The bike accelerated, rocketing over the scarred blacktop on Mountain Avenue, my Keds pedaling furiously in reverse to try to stop it, Roxy's instructions, by now, completely forgotten.

The last thing I heard was Roxy's scream as I reached the bottom of the hill and thundered across River Street, my feet now a blur, past the startled eyes of Red Voisin standing on the corner. He later told my parents that he had never seen anyone pedal so fast *backwards*.

I hit a hump in the blacktop. The bike soared over the edge of the road and into the thicket along the riverbank where the burdock bushes slowed me down. And finally, there I was, bike wheel still spinning, about four feet from the water's edge.

As I sprawled in the bushes, not daring to move for fear of acquiring a few more layers of stinging burdock, I could hear Roxy's screams and someone thrashing through the bushes. Red shouted, "Are you okay?" as he reached me, moved some branches, and pulled the bike away from me. Then he picked me up and carried me up the bank and across the street to the house of Peewee LaPerle, our neighbor and the town garbage collector, who had seen the whole thing. He was still standing on his porch when we got there, shaking his head, a cigar clamped in his teeth. Red deposited me on the porch and went back for the bike. I watched as he and Roxy dragged it from the bushes on the riverbank—the front wheel looking kind of crooked now. Roxy was still crying, not that I blamed her. I didn't feel so cheerful myself. I was going to get it this time.

Roxie went home. Red and Peewee took me into Peewee's house and sat me on the sofa while Buster, Peewee's old German Shepherd, sat nearby and watched with concern. Red took a wet towel and tried to wipe the blood and dirt off my legs. It hurt. When it looked like my legs were as clean as they were going to get, he walked me home to face the music.

We had to buy a new wheel for Roxy's bike, which meant I had to give up my allowance for a while. But my parents were happy that I wasn't killed by any of a number of pick-ups that whizzed down River Street, and that the bushes stopped my headlong course for the river. Roxy's bike looked pretty much like new again, although our friendship had taken a beating.

And as for me—I now had a fresh appreciation for my old, clunky-looking, dependable American bike, with the brakes where they were supposed to be. *New* does not always mean *better*.

You would think that the first thing
a Vermonter with a new driver's license
would do is head south.

Driver's License: Free at Last

My father tried to teach my mother how to drive once, during the summer of 1957. It didn't help that Spike, Ricky, and I were in the backseat of the Desoto, making comments and snickering while my poor mother clutched the steering wheel and drove in circles around the Saxon factory parking lot. "If I have to come back there..." Dad would threaten if we didn't quiet down. But she was just too good a target, my mom, nerves frayed to the breaking point, as she jerked the car forward and then slammed the brakes, tossing us into a pile of arms and legs behind the front seat. "Do it again, Mom!" we'd call. "It's not that hard!" Dad would say, exasperated, "You'll get used to it!"

But she never did, and so never learned how to drive. Maybe she would have if we kids had been old enough to stay home alone for an hour or two.

As for my own driving career, I had apparently inherited Mom's nervous system. It took me two tries in the summer of 1965 to get my license. The man who came from Montpelier once a week to administer the driver's test said I was lucky to get it even then. On my first attempt, I was doing okay, feeling somewhat smug after the uneventful drive around town. Even the parallel parking on Depot

Street went smoothly. Everything was okay until the part where you have to park on a hill, set the brake, and then take off again. I had heard descriptions from the other kids about this being the most difficult part of the test, but most of them had taken the test in cars with standard shifts; this was a 1959 Chrysler with a pushbutton automatic. "It's not that hard," Dad said. "You'll be fine."

The tester had me park halfway up Maple Street. In our town, there was only one street more steep than Maple Street and that was the street we lived on, Mountain Avenue. As we sat on the hill, I released the brake and by mistake pushed the N button, putting the car in *neutral*, instead of *drive*. The car began to roll backwards down Maple, heading for the t-crossing at Depot Street and the A&P parking lot on the other side. *Panic*. Although I had been practicing with my father for months in this same car, I now could not remember how to put the car back in *drive*. As I jerked the handle for the turn signals, trying to find the transmission, and the air rushed faster past the open window, this guy—a tail-gunner on a bomber during World War II—sat calmly next to me, one arm over the back of the seat, as relaxed as if he were in his own Lazy-Boy. We were flying when we passed the American Legion, backwards towards the massive plate glass window that spanned the front of the A&P.

At last, just before we entered the intersection, I remembered to apply the brakes. Regaining some confidence, I remembered about the push buttons. I stopped the car and clicked the transmission into *D*.

Later, I overheard my father wonder aloud to my mother how anyone could flunk a driver's test with a pushbutton automatic. She didn't know, she said. I kept my mouth shut.

Wildlife

I have always liked dogs, but I've never had much luck with them. A German Shepherd bit me when I was four. One minute I'm tumbling and wrestling with Spike on my grandfather's front lawn, the next, I'm wrestling with the dog. Pinned to the ground, I couldn't push him off or roll away. Before I could make sense of it all, my grandfather was there, swinging at the dog with the broom he kept on the front porch.

Another canine mishap occurred the September after my bicycle accident, but this time it was Peewee's dog, Buster, who had the bad luck.

There had been evidence of a skunk in the neighborhood for several nights before the unhappy event. Both Mr. Voisin and Peewee had discovered their garbage cans knocked over and spilled onto their back porches. Then the following night, Buster was barking insistently at the back door so Peewee let him out. The skunk, evidently irritated at having his anticipated buffet interrupted, turned, lifted his tail, and squirted Buster right in the face.

Poor Buster tore off and did the only thing he could do: run like hell to try to get away from his own stench. He bolted down Peewee's back stairs, barking and yelping like a tortured soul. I ran to the screen door to see what all the ruckus was about.

"What's going on?" we asked my father, who was just then getting home from a Knights of Columbus meeting. As he stepped out of the car and looked in the direction of the noise, he was hit by a thundering body of flesh that smelled like the end of the world and mowed him down onto the front seat of the Chrysler. Before he could recover and figure out what had happened, Buster made a desperate, furious run around the interior of the car, and finding no way out except over my father's prostrate body, tore out of the car the way he'd come in, trampling over Dad on the way out.

I stood at the screen door and stared, open-mouthed, the stench by now making it pretty clear what had gotten into, or *onto*, Buster. Poor Buster, his mouth now foaming with revulsion, was still running, back paws sliding, as he bounded up our back stairs, past my astonished eyes, through the screen door I had been too startled to close in time, and into our kitchen.

It was good that the shock made me keep the door open so that Buster, after making a circuit of the living room, could find his way back out again, but not before he spread a fog of overpowering stench around our house. He galloped out the door and soon all we could see was his retreating backside, tail dragging the ground as his paws kicked up September's dust on River Road.

When Peewee finally caught up with him, two days later, poor old Buster was a mess. He'd been rolling in the grass down River Road, swimming in the river, and doing whatever he could to try to get rid of the stink. Even after Peewee had dragged him home and doused him in a tomato juice bath, it took a week or two for the smell to completely dissipate.

As for us, my father had to leave the car windows open for a few days and put some open containers of Arm & Hammer baking soda in there when it was closed up. The house took a lot of Lysol and airing out.

Although it wasn't Buster's fault, the whole incident pretty much put the kibosh to *our* ever getting a dog.

SEPTEMBER

Back to School
with Sears and Roebuck

Shopping for school was simple in St. Froid. We didn't have to walk through endless malls—there weren't any. The *Fall & Winter* Sears Roebuck catalogue was our Macy's and our Jordan Marsh. In a town where you could buy more car mufflers than men's shorts, as my sister once remarked, the catalogue was as much of a lifeline as the A&P.

We were not ambivalent about which of the two Sears' catalogues we preferred. The *Spring & Summer* catalogue when it arrived in mid-January was a welcome reminder that, *yes, Virginia,* summer will return. There was always a sun-splashed cover photo of young girls in pink gingham sundresses, or men in blue and white seersucker suits. On cold, cheerless February evenings when the wind rattled the house and fat flakes of wet snow smacked against the windowpanes, I turned the glossy pages and imagined lying on the beach at Old Orchard, Maine. Or swimming at Indian Pond. Or my mother and father packing up the picnic basket with potato salad and hot dogs, and lemonade in the big Thermos jug, and driving to New Hampshire to see the Old Man of the Mountains. That, by the way, being almost as great an adventure for us kids as Disneyland. When our car rumbled across the dusty iron bridge over the Connecticut River we felt as though we had crossed a border, not a mere state line. New Hampshire took the rugged individualism, the soothing, green rolling landscape, and the ardent patriotism of Vermont and reinterpreted it on steroids. New Hampshire was "live free or die." Hiking trails snaked over craggy mountains, more like the Rockies than the Appalachians, which loomed menacingly and threatened rockslides onto the tiny cars picking their way carefully over the winding roads of Franconia Notch.

But that was the summer catalogue. Sears' *Fall & Winter* catalogue could have waited another six weeks, coming perversely as it did in late July, the best time of year. In high summer, when we played hide 'n' seek in the long summer twilight, it was a disturbing reminder of things to come. So, wearing shorts and t-shirts, picking at the fresh summer scabs on my knees, I waited deep into August before I started looking for my fall wardrobe from the *chubby* section of the catalogue.

There were no real plus sizes back then. Even Sears had, at best, a meager selection: one dress in a tartan plaid—guaranteed to make you look like a draft horse in a blanket; one jumper, a skirt, a cardigan and a navy blue wool coat. The next page showed two slips and some underwear. It was clear that Sears Roebuck considered chubby people to be a minority.

In the end, it would not have mattered what the catalogue offered. I could dream of plaid kilts and creamy white sweaters all I wanted, but the uniform mandated at Mount St. Helene's meant all I was going to get were two navy blue jumpers, two white short-sleeved blouses for every day, one long-sleeved blouse for report card day when Monsignor Breton came to visit, and brown oxfords. Even if I could have worn something more stylish, I would have looked like our Castro-convertible sofa in one of those plaid kilts. Wa-a-a-a-ay too many pleats for a girl whose figure was blossoming into a Kate Smith look-a-like.

The Yankee Law of Natural Retribution

Law #3: If the weather is nice,
we're going to pay for it.

Shoeless in St. Froid

September 1956. The late-afternoon shadows were growing longer and you could hardly walk down River Street without tripping over a squirrel. Despite the satisfying crunch underfoot of the acorns that littered the sidewalk, I hated fall.

September meant back to school—the official end of summer. Labor Day wouldn't be so bleak if summer in Vermont hung around long enough to wear out a bathing suit.

One day in particular stands out in my memory, like a bad dream that would haunt me for a long time. But I didn't know that yet, when I started home from school that afternoon.

It was an unusually warm September that year, temperatures perversely peaking right after Labor Day, just as we started school. Our wool uniforms, never meant to be worn in temperatures over 70 degrees, stuck to the freshly shellacked wooden seats. I was afraid that every time Sister admonished me to sit up straight I would tear the back right off of my uniform. Air conditioning would have been nice, but in a building as old as the convent, we were lucky we had central heat, never mind something as exotic in Vermont as air conditioning, a phenomenon so rare in our part of the world that Brouchette's Diner bragged about it on huge placards in their front windows.

Also, I hated my new shoes: brown leather oxfords that tied with laces, so big and clunky that I felt like Frankenstein's monster.

I felt guilty about this, of course. My parents had spent quite a bit of money on these shoes, keeping a running account at Johnson Brothers' Shoe Store and paying for them a few dollars a week. On Friday nights, my father would stand in line at the People's Bank to cash his check. Then we would walk up the crowded sidewalk of Depot Street, past the blazing store windows, to Sears, and Johnson Brothers, and the Foley Clinic where he would make payments on his accounts. I knew that few of these dollars were spent on shoes for my mother or himself.

Whenever one of us kids needed a new pair, white-haired Mr. Johnson himself would measure our feet in that metal thing that looked like a medieval torture device, and then bring out a pair or two. Then we'd walk our new shoes to the x-ray machine to see how they fit. Now that was a scary thing: I could see my feet right through the shoes. *What could those x-rays be doing to my feet?* After a couple of minutes, when I realized nothing bad was going to happen, I started to think about all the neat stuff you could do with a machine like that; it would be like having Superman's x-ray vision.

That September afternoon, I scuffed along the dusty bridge, almost home, when I felt the sharp stab of a pebble in my shoe. Dropping my bookbag, I bent to untie my shoe, then removed it and started to shake out the pebble. Then, for some reason that to this day makes absolutely no sense, I reached over and shook the shoe over the railing. Seconds later I watched, horrified, as my shoe slipped out of my hand and tumbled into the river. The shoes I hated. A Freudian slip?

I watched in disbelief as the shoe tumbled in slow motion, heel to toe, followed by a soft *kersplash* when it hit the murky water.

My first thought was to jump in after it, but all I could do was the dog paddle. No good. My shoe was gone forever.

My conscience, recognizing something *really* worthy of guilt and remorse, took advantage. It climbed into its pulpit, arms flailing like a southern preacher at a Baptist convention. "Brand new shoes!" it shouted, "not even paid for!"

I stood on tiptoe at the iron railing and considered my options. I could run away from home. But how can you run away when you only have one shoe? Wouldn't people be suspicious of a stranger, a kid with only one shoe? I couldn't go barefoot, winter was coming. I stared down into the muddy water where the shoe had disappeared. The sound of Saxon's factory whistle forced me into action. Dad would be home soon and supper would be on the table. Supper. For the first time that I could remember in my whole, entire life, I had lost my appetite.

I picked up my book bag and turned to walk home, but no matter how desperately I tried to achieve some nonchalance so as not to alarm my parents until I could tell them the whole story, I couldn't amble up River Street, in front of all the neighbors, wearing only one shoe. They would talk. And the most important thing in our town was to keep the neighbors from talking about you. So, I squatted on the bridge again and wrapped a white kerchief, which I kept in my book bag in case we had to go to mass during the school day, around my right foot. There. Maybe they'd think I had a cast on it. I hobbled home as best I could.

As I made the turn to Mountain Avenue and started up the hill, I began to cry. Not just soft whimpers and sniffles, but great heaving, hiccupping sobs as I realized I was only two houses away from having to confess what I had done. There may also have been some primal instinct at play, a kid's natural self-defense that says if you cry, they might take it easy on you.

My mother, wiping her hands on her apron, pushed open the wooden screen door with her hip when she heard my sobs. The door whacked shut as she took one look at my white-wrapped foot, my hobbling gait, and shouted, "Oh my God. She's had an accident! Jimmy, come quick! She's had an accident!"

"Again?" I heard him mutter from behind the *St. Froid Times.*

I wailed even louder as she pulled me against her comforting plaid apron. "What was it," my father asked, "a car? Did someone run over your foot with a car? Stop crying and talk to us!"

Later, after I had regained some composure, and was sure they weren't going to exercise retroactive birth control, I told them what had happened. My father's concern soon turned to disbelief.

"On the bridge? Over the railing? Into the water? What the hell were you thinking—you didn't want to get the bridge dirty?"

Brownies

I was a Girl Scout dropout. It was not entirely my fault. Like Humphrey Bogart in Casablanca, "I was misinformed."

I had admired the Girl Scouts ever since the first time I'd seen them marching in formation in the Fourth of July parade, crisp and strong—yet feminine—in their green and khaki uniforms. I thought that being a Girl Scout would be *cool*. The scarf. The ring. The *adventure*.

Girl Scouts hiked and explored. They camped under the stars and sang Girl Scout songs around a roaring campfire while bears and mountain lions crouched in the shadows just out of range of the firelight. Wow! Sign me up!

However, as it is with other advancements in life, before you could be a Girl Scout you had to be a Brownie, sort of an apprentice Girl Scout. This made sense. The Girl Scouts would not accept just any girl. Hard work and dedication would weed out any fickle glory-seekers who were in it just for the uniform. And the scarf. And the opportunity to march in the Fourth of July parade.

So, my mother took me to a meeting and I registered for Brownies on a golden evening in the fall of 1956. The Brownie Troop Leader was a Mrs. Testerman, a tall woman with an Adam's apple, wearing khaki Bermuda shorts and knee socks. After we signed up, she directed us to buy the uniform and handbook at Harvey's Department Store. Then she asked if there were any questions. I raised my hand and asked her when we'd be going on our first hike. "We'll have to wait for spring, my dear," she answered. Well, of course. What was I thinking?

I wore my new uniform to the next meeting, walking proudly up River Street, flicking dust off the skirt and trying not to get anything on it. We began each meeting by studying the Girl Scout manual. Then we would start a project.

By the following spring, none of our projects had yet involved The Wilderness or The Great Outdoors. My parents had bought me a sleeping bag for Christmas, but the only place I had slept with it so far had been under the kitchen table. Meanwhile, in Brownies, we continued to glue macaroni and alphabet-soup pasta letters onto pieces of wood to spell out things like the Girl Scout motto, "Be Prepared."

I asked Mrs. Testerman again, sometime in May, when we would be camping out and she said, "As soon as the ground warms up enough, you know."

I had run out of patience so I quit. But later that summer, I finally realized my dreams of sleeping in the wilderness and gathering around a campfire in a simpler, more informal way: with my cousins, in the woods, behind Uncle John's camp.

The Bind That Ties

On summer nights in those days there were record hops across the river in the parking lot of Harvey's Department Store. I would sit at my open bedroom window, listen to the music and imagine those lucky girls in their poodle skirts and ponytails, swinging to The Everly Brothers' "Wake Up, Little Susie" and "The Great Pretender" by The Platters.

It was 1959. I was eleven and could not imagine ever being old enough to go to the dances—sixteen seemed so far off. I would probably never be thin enough to wear a poodle skirt, either. Later, as I flipped my pillow to the cooler side and drifted off to sleep to the sound of crickets—real ones, not Buddy Holly's group—I thought about asking my mother for a girdle. It might make me thin enough for a poodle skirt and would have the added benefit that I could stop wearing knee socks, which, regardless of how new they were, would creep down my calves, worm their way into my oxfords, and lie there puddled around my ankles. I had tried everything, even rubber bands that broke and one time almost sling-shotted Sister Cecilia in the knee during Glee Club. I wanted to wear nylon stockings and for that you needed either a garter belt or a girdle.

My mother resisted at first, saying I was too young, but later admitted that she had started wearing one at about my same age. So she gave in.

We bought it on a Saturday in September at The Rose Shoppe (Ladies and Little Miss Ready-to-Wear – Millinery – Lingerie – Hosiery). When it came to shopping, these truly were "the good old days." You could stand in a dressing room in the back of the store and someone would bring you clothes to try. You didn't have to traipse around the store in the dress you had just pulled over your head, tag hanging off, worried that someone would take your stuff out of the dressing room.

Rose herself, smelling of My Sin dusting powder, helped us that day. She was a very nice woman with hennaed hair and a chest that I envied: it arrived a minute or two before she did. Four years later she was to give me my first real job that wasn't a babysitting job: vacuuming and dusting the store and assembling the black and gold Rose Shoppe boxes that they put your purchases in back then. She also would let me make my first charge account purchase for a black and white checked Jantzen bathing suit with molded plastic cups that made me look like Jayne Mansfield. I had to be careful, though, not to let anyone come too close. If someone hugged me the cups would push in like a crushed Dixie cup and, if I didn't notice, would stay pushed in—my chest collapsed like a deflated hot air balloon—while I lolled obliviously by the pool.

Anyways, in the dressing room, I stripped off my dungarees and Rose brought me a girdle to try on. *How do you breathe in these things?* I wondered. It wasn't a panty girdle, just the regular bandage style, garters dangling from the bottom and pressing small dents into the tops of my thighs. A roll of pink flesh mushed out over the top and circled my waist like an inflated hula-hoop.

Rose suggested I needed a larger size.

We eventually left the store with the girdle wrapped in tissue paper in a Rose Shoppe box, like a birthday gift, along with two pair of nylon stockings in a flat, blue box. Lingerie was treated with respect in those days—no gimmicky plastic eggs.

With my bedroom door firmly closed, I tried the girdle on again after we got home and slipped my school uniform on over it. It was miraculous: the girdle smoothed out and flattened my tummy and hips. If only my mother would let me wear it to school. But I knew she wouldn't.

I could try to slip it on in the morning, but my mother, upstairs making beds and getting ready for work, could easily catch me putting it on. Even with practice, it took a few minutes to tug it up over my cotton underwear.

But what if I was already wearing it under my nightgown? Then I could just jump out of bed, pull the nightgown off, pull the blouse and jumper over my head and she'd never know I had it on. To save time and reduce the possibility of getting caught, I would sleep with my blouse and undershirt under my nightgown, too.

I wore the girdle to mass on Sunday with the nylon stockings and my black patent-leather Easter shoes. I'm sure lots of people, like Bobby DuBois, for instance, noticed how good I looked. When we got home, it went into my dresser. But then, on Sunday night, I slipped it back on along with a white short-sleeved blouse, under my plaid flannel nightgown, and went to bed.

I awoke every couple of hours to pull the girdle back down from where it had crept up to my waist like the rubbery link between two hot dogs.

My blouse was wrinkled by morning but that was no big deal—only the sleeves and Peter Pan collar ever showed under my uniform. Walking to school, Patsy observed that I looked different. She asked me if my legs hurt. The truth was that with no stockings attached to keep it firmly anchored over my hips the girdle tended to ride up. I had visions of it riding up and snapping me at the waist like a window shade with a bad spring. To compensate, I took smaller, mincing steps.

It was not a good morning. I spent most of it in the bathroom pulling the damn thing down. Plus, I was still wearing knee-highs so between them rolling down and this thing rolling up, I was ready to go home by lunchtime. Sister Mary Margaret pulled me aside right after lunch and my fourth trip to the girls' room and asked me if I had *le vavite*. Diarrhea! My salvation! She had just given me the perfect out. "Oui," I lied.

By the time I hobbled home at 1 o'clock, thighs stinging, I had had that contraption on for about 18 hours and I was getting pretty darn sick of it. In fact, I had just about decided that I was never going to wear it again, stockings or no stockings.

I was saved, in 1965, by the invention of panty hose.

OCTOBER

Dad's Cold War

The smell of burning leaves. A leaden sky bearing down on us, seeming low enough to touch. We watch a flock of wild geese, high above, sailing toward the gray southern horizon. *They're lucky,* I think, *escaping the coming winter.* Spike, Ricky, and I stand on the back lawn on a raw October morning, clutching rakes like the farmers in a painting by Grant Wood. Temps are in the mid-40s but we are warm in our plaid flannel shirts as long as we keep moving and that's exactly what my father wants us to do. We are helping him rake leaves to burn, the burning part being the most fun.

It was a typical October Saturday afternoon, this one in 1960 when I was twelve, my brothers were ten and eight, and my sister would soon celebrate her first birthday. Our favorite television show that year was *Route 66*, bringing back memories of our family adventure, seven years earlier, when my father had made *his* attempt to escape the Vermont winters.

Like many other folks in those post-war years, my father packed us up and joined the caravan of World War II veterans and their families migrating to Los Angeles in search of prosperity and, in his case, a less robust climate. What he found instead was that it was better to put up with the New England weather than to live three thousand miles away from the rest of the family. So we returned to Vermont six months later.

But the trip was, in many ways, the trip of a lifetime. On a September morning in 1953, we made a tearful exit from St. Froid, waving goodbye to Grammy and Grampy, who looked tiny and lonely on their big white porch, behind the dying hydrangeas. We were ten days on the road, up hill both ways—the Rockies on the way out, the Appalachians on the way back—Dad driving a brand new 1952 half-ton Chevy truck. We drove west and eventually reached St. Louis where we picked up Route 66, which took us all the way to Santa Monica. I remember Joplin, Missouri: a television in our room, the first one I had ever seen; you had to put in a quarter for a half-hour's viewing. Gallup, New Mexico: tiny cabins along the sun-baked road. Hot southwestern diners, onions frying, twisted rolls of fly paper fluttering in the futile draft of the ceiling fan where waitresses in white uniforms with their names on the pockets pulled out highchairs for Ricky. We sat up all night through a sandstorm near Amarillo, Texas, my parents stuffing rags under the doorjamb and windowsills to keep the sand from sifting in. In Holbrook, Arizona, we slept in concrete wigwams. The truck had a couple of flat tires and once, an overheated radiator in the Arizona desert. My mother almost wore out her rosary beads.

The whole adventure would have killed a lesser man than my father but he always spoke wistfully of those days on the road and of southern California where it never snows. And every winter, when we settled into the deep freeze, he'd say, "We should've stayed in California."

So that overcast Saturday afternoon in 1960, as I watched my father rake leaves, I began to appreciate how much of his life was spent in getting ready for, and coping with, a typical Vermont winter.

Dad's Top Five Tips for Getting Your House Through a Vermont Winter

Cold War Hint #1: Choose Your Ammunition Wisely

Once my father realized that there would be no escape from the dreaded cold, he drew up his battle plans. The first skirmish occurred in the fall of 1956, the beginning of our first winter in the old house on Mountain Avenue. There was an ancient coal-burning furnace in the dirt-floored cellar, so big and so inefficient that it could chomp through a ton of coal like an AARP convention through a free salad bar. He spent most of that first winter trudging up and down the rickety cellar stairs every couple of hours to shovel coal into the furnace like a stoker on the *Titanic*, his efforts almost as futile.

"You couldn't control the temperature," he told Uncle Joe one time, "It would get so hot, why...it would drive you right out of the house. Then before you knew it, she'd cool right off again."

He never got a break from this thing. Even on Saturday nights, while we watched *Your Hit Parade* and *Jackie Gleason*, sometime during the evening my father would push himself out of his chair and head for the cellar. After a few minutes, the clang of the furnace door echoed through the cast-iron grate in the living room floor, followed by the rattle of coal hitting a steel shovel and the staccato of muffled expletives, the only time we heard him curse, except for when he put the lights on the Christmas tree.

In the spring of 1957, he bought an oil burner, a 300-gallon oil tank, and a Honeywell thermostat. This marked the end of the first battle.

But even after the first oil delivery for the new furnace—300 gallons at 18 cents a gallon—it was clear that our old house was still not going to be a cheap date, no matter how you tried to warm her up. So by the following Labor Day, my father had stockpiled his supplies and begun to erect his defenses.

Cold War Hint #2: Call in Reinforcements

We had a kerosene stove in the kitchen to supplement the furnace for the coldest part of the winter. Dad hauled it out of the back closet and set it up about the middle of October. It served double duty, keeping the kitchen warm, and giving my mother a convenient place to simmer soups and stews. She also had a small black metal oven, about a foot square with a thermometer in the door, which they placed on top of the stove. It was open at the bottom to capture the heat from the burner—this is where she baked her beans all day Saturday, the aroma of maple syrup and salt pork enough to drive you wild by mid-afternoon.

Cold War Hint #3: Protecting the Borders

On a Saturday in October, Dad would take the screens off the windows, then haul the storm windows out of the basement. He and my mother would wash them with ammonia water and newspapers until they squeaked. They were heavy, wood-framed windows so installing them in the upstairs windows took some doing. Dad would climb the old wooden ladder, hauling a window up with him like a circus performer, and heave it up against the sill of the open window where my mother, or later my brothers, grabbed the hooks from the inside and clicked them into the eyebolts on the sills. Fourteen windows in all.

Cold War Hint #4: More Reinforcements

He taped clear plastic onto the insides of some of the windows. The downside was that there were only three or four windows in our house that you could see through clearly all winter. The rest of them offered a blurry world, as if seen through a smear of Vaseline.

Cold War Hint #5: Cover Your Bases

The walls of the old house were not insulated, so by mid-February it was common for the electrical outlets to be coated in a layer of frost. So my father wrapped the entire foundation in a skirt of black tarpaper, held in place with furring strips nailed just under the clapboards. By early November, the house was wrapped up tight like an Easter basket in cellophane. Even when the wind whistled through the electrical wires on the pole near the front porch, and the snow drifted three feet deep around the foundation, we kids could sprawl on the green carpet in the living room to watch television and never feel a draft through those old walls.

Trivia question for baby boomers:

Who the heck was *The Wild Man of Borneo?*
My mother often said we looked like him,
but I don't remember ever seeing a picture
of him, not even in *Life* magazine.

Halloween in St. Froid

Halloween was on a Monday in 1960. On Saturday, we still hadn't decided what to wear. Mom and Dad had suggested some television personalities—Davy Crockett, Superman, Sergeant Preston of the Yukon, the Mouseketeers—but they all seemed like too much work. So predictably, we would wind up with the same costumes as the year before, and the year before that: I went as a gypsy, and the boys went as hobos, with burnt cork rubbings on their cheeks.

But this year, perhaps due to my emerging puberty, I decided on something more feminine. I wanted to look like Disney's Cinderella, when she went to the ball. Mom offered me a pink dress of hers, one with a full skirt, and I had about a bushel of pop-beads I could use to dress it up. My mother and I worked on it all day Saturday and by the time we sat down to our beans and franks, it was perfect: I was going to be *beautiful*. Yup.

Halloween night arrived and the thermometer on the back porch read only 41 degrees, but after a quick supper of Campbell's tomato soup and grilled Velveeta sandwiches, I was ready to go. I climbed the stairs to my room to change my clothes and there was the dress, on a hanger dangling from my bedroom door, glittering in the dark like

Cinderella's ball gown. We had stitched some nylon net to the inside of the skirt so it would puff out, sewed sequins to the bodice, and pinned strands of pearly pink pop beads around the skirt. There were a few more strings of beads to wear around my neck and a pair of rhinestone earrings. It was important to me, this Halloween when I was twelve, to look pretty. And there was no doubt that in this costume I would.

After checking myself again in the full-length mirror I flounced down the stairs where my brothers stood by the back door, quick to remind me that our real mission was not to win a masquerade contest but to go out and haul in as much candy as possible. And, based on past experience, we knew that if we didn't get out there early enough some other kids would get all the Three Musketeers and Snickers bars and we'd be left with *apples*. We even used old pillowcases as trick-or-treat sacks, in case of a record haul.

We'd almost made it out the back door when my mother called me back, "You're not going out there like that, are you?"

I knew it was too good to be true. "Like what?" I asked.

"With no coat on," my father added.

"Maybe I don't need one?" I asked, knowing it was hopeless. "No one's going to see my costume if I wear my coat over it!"

My mother came to the rescue. "How about wearing the coat *under* the costume—the dress has an elastic waist. It has a lot of give."

I took off the dress, put on my plaid wool jacket and put the gown back on over it. The dress's zipper now went only about halfway up the back. I checked my reflection in the kitchen window: Cinderella had morphed into her Fairy Godmother. Bibbidi-bobbidi-boo.

Another Halloween ruined by the cold. My father was right—we should have stayed in California.

NOVEMBER

Grampy Makes Boudin

The French are not a particularly bloodthirsty people, if you don't count *la guillotine*. But then, it was a physician who invented it as a more humane method of execution than the more traditionally used axe. Generally, the French would rather make love and drink wine than kill each other. Uncharacteristically for such a peace-loving people, things got bloody in the fall when my grandparents made boudin.

Grampy, my mother's father, looked like Fred Mertz. He wore suspenders to hold up his pants and a flat-billed cap on his bald head, like the newsboys in gangster movies *"Extra, Extra, Read all about it!"* When we asked him what had happened to his hair he would answer that my grandmother had hit him on the head with a frying pan, which we knew was ridiculous because Grammy would never hit anyone with a frying pan or anything else.

Grampy also liked to entertain us kids by jiggling his false teeth around in his mouth until they were upside down, the uppers where the lowers should be and vice versa. Then he'd smile and we'd scream; there was something so Jeckyl-and-Hyde about this transformation.

I was secretly convinced that I was his favorite grandchild, being the second one and the first girl. I rode along blissfully beside him wherever he wanted to take me. We had even shared a near-death experience on a hot August afternoon in 1949, when I was a toddler in a car seat. His big black 1946 Buick stalled at the railroad crossing on Miller Street, just as the flashing red lights and bells sounded the oncoming train. He grabbed me with the car seat and lunged out, just clearing the tracks as the screeching diesel rammed into the side of his car, pushing it about a quarter mile down the track, like a Holstein on a cowcatcher. The engineer knew my grandfather and recognized the car; the man retired shortly thereafter. And Grampy and I had made the front page of the *St. Froid Times*, which made me a sort of celebrity, but I was too young to appreciate it.

Anyway, back to the boudin. He took me with him to pick up pig blood at the slaughterhouse, the November when I was eight years old, to make *boudin*, a sausage made since olden times by French farmers. In olden days, they slaughtered their pigs in the fall and preserved the meat for the winter—preserving everything but the *oink*, my grandfather used to say.

Grampy knew a lot about meat, having worked as a meat cutter for years at Charlie's IGA on the corner of Concord Avenue and Pittsford Street. While my grandfather was alive, my mother never had to actually trek through the grocery store. She would call Charlie's on Friday morning, order her groceries, and Grampy delivered them late Friday afternoon. And being Grampy, he always included a surprise. Once it was small sample boxes of a new cereal called AlphaBits; another time he opened a cardboard box in the middle of the kitchen floor and out crawled a lobster, its claws clicking across the linoleum and terrorizing us kids as we alternated between running away from it and approaching it on our hands and knees.

So on Friday nights in the fall and winter, my grandparents made the sausage to sell in the store the following week. I had heard about this, but until that day when we went to the slaughterhouse, it never occurred to me that *boudin*—blood sausage—was exactly that and made from real blood; I thought it was just a name. But, then, I didn't know that *tongue* was a real cow's tongue, either.

We drove to the meatpacking plant by the railroad tracks in Lincolnville, a building that resembled the barn on Uncle Steve's farm. Grampy opened the trunk and pulled out a big empty milk can and we walked up the short wooden stairs to a dock where men stood around in denim overalls and Ralston-Purina caps, smoking cigarettes. Waiting to pick up their blood, I guess. Grampy dropped off the can and walked up to another one that was full. I looked down inside and there was no doubt that it was filled to the brim with real blood.

Once we got back to Grampy's house and they started making the sausage, I forgot all about being squeamish and just watched. I did enjoy eating it, after all, if I didn't think about where it came from…sliced thick and fried in a cast iron skillet.

I insert this recipe for posterity, not because you might be interested in making it. But, then again, you never know. I ate some at a little bistro in Quebec City a few years back and it was as good as I remembered it.

Recipe for Boudin

- 2 cups pork blood, salted
- 2 lbs. fresh pork
- 5 onions, chopped
- cloves
- Summer Savory
- coriander seeds, crushed
- 2 Tbsp. flour
- salt and pepper

Place fresh pork in a large pot and add enough water to cover. Add salt and 3 chopped onions. Simmer for 3 hours. Remove the meat from the cooking liquid and let it cool. Cut the meat into very small pieces or grind with meat grinder. Add meat to the cooking liquid with the 2 remaining onions, pepper, and spices. Bring liquid to a boil and slowly add the blood by pouring it through a sieve. Stir constantly. Add the flour mixed with small amount of water. The flour may be browned in the oven before adding to the meat, provided that slightly more flour is used. Simmer the mixture on low heat for approximately 1 half hour, stirring frequently.

To make the sausages: Clean the small intestines of a pig, cut into 20-inch pieces and tie at one end. Using a funnel (the Acadian tradition called for a piece of birch bark), fill the intestines with the sauce until the intestine is three quarters full. Press out the air and tie the other end, leaving some space for expansion. Put the sausages in boiling water and cook for 45 minutes to 1 hour.

Slice and brown in a frying pan, preferably a cast-iron skillet, before serving.

How They Met

My parents used to wonder why I always took to the couch with a hot water bottle after spending a weekend at my grandparents' house. It might have been the vanilla-ice-cream-and-ginger-ale floats, as many as I wanted; or the slabs of warm bread and peanut butter; or my grandmother's homemade donuts and pies. I don't know. It certainly wasn't because my grandmother was a bad cook.

I often think of my grandmother as I grow older and reflect on how hard she worked all her life. She baked bread to sell during the Great Depression, dozens of loaves every week, often sharing what she made with the hobos who stopped by the screen door and asked for a handout. She didn't stop baking when the Depression ended because hard on the heels of bad times came World War II.

Even into her fifties, she would rise before dawn to mix the batter in a large galvanized washtub used only for that purpose. I would often spend the weekend at my grandmother's, in what had been my own mother's bedroom and still smelled of Lifebuoy soap and Jergen's lotion, and I would get up as soon as I heard Grammy moving about the kitchen.

She was a small woman so my grandfather had made a stool out of a tree stump for her to stand on, so she could reach deep down into the washtub on the kitchen table to knead the dough, her forearms white with flour. She bought King Arthur flour in 100-pound cotton sacks that she and my mother would recycle into bed sheets. Until I was a teenager and my grandmother grew too old to bake, I slept with a picture of King Arthur in the middle of my bed.

She shaped the dough into balls, each the size of a grapefruit, two to a loaf pan, then brushed them with milk so they would brown. When they were done, each loaf was wrapped in waxed paper and tied with string. When she was a girl, during the Depression, my mother helped her wash the baking pans and then delivered the golden loaves with her wagon.

My grandmother's own mother died when she was nine years old. Her father, a dour man with a mustache like a walrus, married a woman with two daughters. My grandmother became a real-life Cinderella: mean stepmother, two mean stepsisters—the whole darn package.

When she turned fourteen, Grammy left her home in Quebec and came to work as a housemaid for a well-to-do family in our town. She wore a black uniform with a long white apron and a cap. The wealthy woman was kind and taught my grandmother how to entertain with individual silver salt and pepper shakers at each place setting, place cards, linen napkins and gleaming silverware. And as she learned these things, Grammy wondered if she would ever have her own home, her own dining room with crystal serving bowls and silver platters, place cards, and soup tureens.

The handsome funny man who became my grandfather was apprenticed to a butcher where Grammy shopped for fresh roasts and chops. And so they met and fell in love, and Grammy's dream came true.

In black-and-white photographs, they stand, side by side at the head of their table, their five children gathered around them, and she serves her bread and pickles, baked beans, *boudin*, tourtiere or stuffed turkey. And, somehow, you can tell as you gaze at the photograph, that as far as she was concerned, all the hard work was worth it. "Life," she used to say, "is what you make it."

December is the only month whose
weather usually does not
disappoint Vermonters:
It is winter. It is cold. And it snows.

DECEMBER

Christmas in St. Froid, 1961

The holidays are tough on teenagers. The change in routine interrupts the lifeline of telephone calls and hanging out at the skating rink. And that *call of the wild* makes it hard to stay home, days at a stretch, all alone, with no one but your parents and your brothers and sisters and an occasional aunt or uncle for company.

Puberty is hell, the age when it dawns on you one morning, as you look in the bathroom mirror, that if you don't do something about it, and soon, YOU'RE GOING TO LOOK LIKE YOUR PARENTS! The same young girl who a year ago couldn't wait to look like her mother is suddenly horrified at the thought. This explains why teenagers sometimes go to extremes to look and dress as little like "the old man" and "the old lady" as possible.

And although it's an exciting time, growing up sometimes feels like you're giving up more than you're getting, or so it seemed to me that Christmas of 1961, just before my fourteenth birthday. The epiphany came in early November when my mother asked what I wanted for Christmas, adding, "I guess you won't be asking for toys anymore."

I was uncharacteristically speechless. For the first time I realized the irrevocability of it: my life marching forward to high school and college and marriage and babies and death.

Once you give up toys, there's no turning back.

I would be in high school next year at this time but I wasn't ready. I was still waiting to grow breasts, the only female on both sides of my family to not have any. My neighbor, Celine Voisin, the same age as I, had some. Big ones. She also wore short skirts and had mastered the art of creating the perfect flip in her hair, lacquered in place with gallons of Aqua Net. I envied her; she was comfortable around boys. We were both French, but where she had inherited the flirty, sidelong glance from *her* gene pool, I had received the Gallic temper and big butt from mine. And boys made me uneasy, especially high school boys who shaved their faces, scratched their privates, and smoked cigarettes. My high school future did not look good.

I was scared to grow up, to grow away to some place else that wasn't *here*, to somewhere that wasn't *home*, as a new and surprising affection for this hick town grew in me. I felt the door to my childhood about to slam shut behind me, and it opened only one way. This made all of the traditions more poignant that Christmas of 1961, from the first elf in the Christmas Parade to the last notes at midnight mass.

Traditions

That Christmas season, Peewee LaPerle played Santa again in the Christmas parade on the Saturday after Thanksgiving, and we felt fortunate to have such a celebrity for a neighbor. He had a real beard that he Halo-shampooed into a burst of fluff. Riding down Depot Street, perched on a throne on the back of the St. Froid Fire Department hook and ladder truck, Peewee appreciated as no one else could the aroma of fresh-cut pine instead of swill. There must have been a thousand of us kids in Depot Square, wrapped in scarves and stamping our feet, scrambling for the peppermint candy he tossed from his sleigh as the St. Froid Town Band, established in 1830, played "Here Comes Santa Claus" and "Rudolph the Red-Nosed Reindeer."

That same afternoon was the Saxon's Wagon and Scale Work's Christmas party, held every year in the auditorium at St. Froid Academy, the only place big enough to hold all the kids whose parents worked at Saxon's. Saxon's Employee's Activities Club spent weeks organizing the party. There was entertainment: cartoons, a ventriloquist, and St. Froid's only rock-and-roll singer, who did a pretty nifty impersonation of Elvis. At that age, though, I had yet to appreciate his gyrations. And every kid got a present, a real toy, appropriate for our age and sex, shopped for and wrapped by the hardworking members of the Activities Club, along with a colorful box of animal crackers and ribbon candy.

Trees

On the Sunday after the party, Dad reluctantly handed us his saw and some rope and we would hike, Spike, Ricky and I, down snow-covered River Road, looking for a Christmas tree. I don't know if the trees we harvested belonged to anyone—it was hard to tell in those vast snowy fields. At least we didn't do what George, Red Voisin's youngest brother, did. When Mr. Voisin had sent him out for a Christmas tree, George, not in the mood to trek all the way down River Road, had gone up Mountain Avenue to Roxanne's house and hacked down a fir tree on their front lawn. And not just any of the fir trees on their front lawn, but the one right in the middle of a perfect row. Then George, whose brainpower exhibited the wattage of a Christmas bulb, dragged it down the hill and propped it up against the front of his own house. The police found it there the next morning.

As for our mission, Dad gave us the same warning every year: *a tree always looks smaller in the wild than it does in the house; if it's longer than the toboggan,* **find another one!** Many years, many trees; some that Dad had had to cut about two feet off of to get into the house. One year we hauled home a *cat-piss pine* that smelled like stale beer after it warmed up in the living room.

Gifts

We decided to buy a color television for my parents that year, convinced that the only reason we didn't already have one was because they were just too busy to go shopping for one, working as they did two jobs apiece in those days. So we pooled what remained of our birthday money, my babysitting receipts and Spike's paper route and met at Sears Roebuck one afternoon after school. As we fingered the price tags on the Zeniths and Motorolas, most in the neighborhood of $600, it became clear why there weren't any color televisions in our neighborhood: only millionaires could afford them. We went to Woolworth's where we found some handkerchiefs: pink embroidered linen for my mother, plaid cotton for Dad.

Christmas Eve and Tourtiere

Early on Christmas Eve, we played checkers at the kitchen table, drank ginger ale, and listened to Christmas music on the radio. Now and then Dan Sweeney would break in with a news bulletin that an unidentified flying object had been spotted by Air Force radar about eight miles northeast of St. Froid. It appeared to be a sleigh and eight tiny reindeer.

By nine o'clock, we were taking naps so we could stay awake for midnight mass and for the party afterwards—the traditional French Reveillon. At Reveillon, we ate *tourtiere* (meat pie), date-nut bread, and homemade sweet mixed pickles. And a cocktail or two for the grown-ups. A study conducted back then would have shown that most French Canadians who died in the winter were stricken on Christmas morning, the result of eating *tourtiere* after Midnight mass. Those Canucks who survived then lived into their hundreds.

Ribbon Candy and Walnuts in the Shell

On Christmas Day I woke to the sight of one of my father's huge cotton work socks, freshly laundered and bulging with goodies, hanging on the foot of my bed, and with a sense of relief that I wasn't too old for a Christmas stocking. Ricky and Spike were already rifling through the contents of their stockings, which they had dumped on their beds. I could tell by the sound of it that they were already getting into Necco Wafers and Sky Bars so I went in and sat on the edge of Ricky's bed and opened mine. I pulled out Tangee lipstick—which took on a different shade depending on your skin color—nail polish, a circle pin in a tiny black box, two rolls of Lifesavers, Boston Baked Beans candy, a box of Jordan almonds—my favorite movie candy— walnuts in the shell, and some Teaberry chewing gum. And, in the toe, the traditional orange—a treat that we didn't get year around.

There was something decadent about munching ribbon candy and candy bars before breakfast as we waited for Mom and Dad to get their coffee. It was the only day of the year we could get away with it.

The morning went on, the mound of gifts giving way to mounds of crumpled gift wrap. Mom and Dad liked what we gave them, doing well to hide their inevitable disappointment when they learned that we had meant to buy them a color television.

Later, while my brothers rooted under the tree to make sure we hadn't missed anything, my father handed me a package with a tag that read *From Daddy*. Puzzled—our gifts always said from *Santa* or *Love, Mom and Dad*—I opened the box to find, swaddled in tissue paper, a doll. My last doll.

While I had been moaning about getting older and what I was giving up, my father had been listening. In his thoughtful way, he was letting me know that no matter how old I got, I'd always be his little girl.

Recipe for Tourtiere

To make one meat pie:

♦ 1 pound of ground pork – medium lean
♦ 1 small onion, chopped
♦ ½ tsp. salt
♦ ¼ tsp. celery salt
♦ ½ cup water
♦ ¼ to ½ cup unseasoned bread crumbs
♦ pastry of your choice, enough for a 2-crust pie

Place all ingredients except crumbs in a saucepan. Bring to a boil and cook uncovered for 20 minutes over medium heat. Remove from heat and add a few spoonfuls of crumbs. Let stand for 10 minutes. If the fat is sufficiently absorbed by the crumbs, do not add more crumbs. If not, continue to add crumbs until the fat is absorbed.

Cool and pour into a pastry-lined pie plate. Cover with crust. Bake at 400° until golden brown, 20-30 minutes. Serve hot. A cooked tourtiere can be frozen 4 or 5 months. It does not have to be thawed before reheating.

An Angel We Have
Heard on High

Ribbon candy. Gifts tied in curling ribbon. But to me, midnight mass was the best part of Christmas. Although I was the only member of our family who did not contribute to the services, I was an appreciative audience. Uncle George sang "O Holy Night" in a rich tenor so moving that grown men pulled large, white linen handkerchiefs from their back pockets and dabbed at their eyes, memories of childhood Christmas Eves suddenly coming to life in the incensed air around them. The organist was Aunt Rose, Uncle George's wife, who sat on the oak bench, dwarfed by the massive pipes of the organ that soared into the darkness above the choir loft. I used to sit at mass, turn and stare at the pipes, and wonder where they stopped: in heaven?

Our family was well represented in the choir, too, including Mom and Dad. Spike sang in the boys' choir and Ricky was an altar boy. So I usually sat in a pew with my grandparents, trying to sit still and follow in the missal I had received for First Communion.

But Christmas Eve 1959 was different. During that eleventh year of my life, I lost a grandfather and gained a sister.

Growing Up Cold

Grampy died on the eighth of May, and I learned what it meant to have a broken heart. From the moment I was called away from the fifth-grade class, I was inconsolable.

But it's funny how things work out. In my grief during the funeral, I did not recognize that my mother's navy blue, two-piece dress—worn with a hat with a veil over her eyes—was a maternity dress. I overheard only later during the luncheon at our house that she was going to have a baby. A baby! Maybe, at last, I would have a sister! I prayed for a sister for five long months and finally, on Sunday afternoon, October 18, my sister Cecile—whom we called Cissy—was born.

So, Christmas 1959 was certainly going to be very different. Grampy was gone and there was a new baby sister in our house.

I sat with Grammy and Aunt Aileen at midnight mass. Dad was in the choir and my mother had had to stay home with two-month-old Cissy. The jingle-bell sound of boot buckles echoed from the rafters as people filed into church and stamped the snow off their feet. Removing their gloves, they dipped icy fingers into the holy water font and wished their neighbors Merry Christmas in loud whispers. Then the organ thrummed into tune, heralding the carol singing before mass. "Les anges dans nos campagnes" and "Il est ne le divin enfant," we sang.

As the three huge bronze bells in the steeple tolled midnight, Uncle George sang "O Holy Night" in French—"Minuit Chretien"—the language in which it had been written. Fall on your knees, people, your Savior is born!

Later, at communion, I jumped up to move into the crowded aisle in front of my grandmother when the music started and a voice began to sing Schubert's "Ave Maria." That voice. . .like an *angel*. The sound of shuffling feet quieted as the people returned from communion and looked up at the choir loft, at the boy in the red cassock and white surplice, who stood with folded hands at the rail.

I had never heard the church so still. As the congregation took communion and moved quietly back to their seats, their eyes never left the boy in the choir. I craned my neck to look, too, and there in

175

the front of the choir stood my brother Spike, freckles faded since last summer, cowlick temporarily Bryl-Creamed into submission.

I have never heard "Ave Maria" sung again since that night without remembering my brother, the untamed boy who was transformed into an angel that Christmas Eve.

New Year's

New Year's belongs to the beginning of the year, but it is part of the Christmas holiday and so my memories of New Year's are inseparable from those of Christmas.

On New Year's morning, following an old French tradition, we asked for my father's blessing. We knelt before him, each our turn, and he made the sign of the cross on our foreheads with the thumb of his right hand, the same hand that in the coming months would pull our loosened baby teeth, weld bars of steel, grip hammers and paintbrushes, shovels, and wrenches. He blessed us.

And we were, without a doubt, truly blessed.

The Piano

The piano moved in on a Saturday afternoon in the summer of 1956 when I was eight, and my life would never be the same. My mother's great-aunt Robertine gave it to us. She was an accomplished pianist and musical composer and had published many pieces for piano, but now her arthritic hands could no longer play. It must have broken her heart to give it up.

Just getting the big mahogany upright into the house was a feat. You couldn't go up the front stairs, which were closer to the living room, because they were too steep, so my father and two of my uncles rolled it off the truck onto a ramp they had placed on the back stairs and then rolled it through the kitchen and into the living room. When they were done and it was in place, my mother sat down and played "Whispering," one of the pieces she could still play from memory. Like Aunt Robertine, my mother also had studied piano for many years and though she always protested that she was a little rusty, it came back to her as she ran her fingers over the keys.

The piano was 42 years old that summer, having been built in the spring of 1914, something I learned many years later when my husband refinished it. Each piano key is a curved piece of wood, about a foot long, with ivory covering only about the first six inches of it.

Growing Up Cold

The artisan who assembled it had written the date in pencil along the side of a key, the letters still just as fresh as they had been on April 6, 1914.

I started trying to play the piano almost as soon as it hit the door. *Oh boy*, I thought. Maybe I could play honky-tonk like Joanne Castle on the Lawrence Welk show. Or "Big Band" music, like Uncle Lennie, an old friend of the family. Uncle Lennie, an Irishman who looked like Jimmy Cagney, played the piano bars in Boston. It looked relatively easy, unlike a guitar or a saxophone: on a piano the notes were right there in front of you—all you had to do was find them.

And so, I picked at the keys after school and on Sundays after mass while we waited for my mother to put the chicken or roast pork on the table. It wasn't loud enough to me, so I took the front panels off. Besides, it looked more honky-tonk that way and I liked to watch the hammers bouncing along as I played.

A year or two later I read in a magazine that you could make your piano sound authentically honky-tonk by putting thumbtacks on the face of each hammer where it strikes the piano string. So I tried it: eighty-eight thumbtacks, one at a time.

I was surprised that my parents let me do that—put thumbtacks on the hammers—but maybe it was because something had changed by then: I was actually playing the darn thing. Recognizable melodies. *By ear*, they called it.

I tried to mimic Joanne Castle, playing along with her record album on the hi-fi, songs like "That Old Gang of Mine" and "My Gal Sal." I tried popular tunes like "The Chipmunk Song" and "Last Date." True, my chording left a lot to be desired, and I could only play in the key of C, but my parents were impressed anyway. I was finally doing something that they could be proud of, that didn't involve sprained ankles or visits to the Foley Clinic.

And so, as parents do, they got excited: visions of Carnegie Hall danced in their heads. Maybe I'd have the professional musical career that they had both longed for. So, they signed me up for piano lessons.

Mrs. Jacobs soon had me practicing my fingering, doing scales, and learning chords. I practiced marches and some waltzes, but

179

nothing that even remotely sounded like honky-tonk piano. Classical music didn't suit me. Somehow, I couldn't see myself seated at a grand piano where men in tuxedos and women in black cocktail dresses sipped martinis.

After I whined enough, my parents, reluctantly, let me quit. So I went back to my thumbtacked piano in the living room of our house, closed the door, removed the front, and pounded on those keys until the windows rattled.

While I was looking for *cool* in all the wrong places, I played the piano every day. After a time, my parents asked me to play whenever our relatives got together. Aunts and uncles crowded around the old piano, glass in one hand, cigarette in the other, potato chips and French onion dip on the coffee table, and we sang. Those were great times, persuading my father to sing "I'll Never Smile Again," while Uncle Bill, in a wheelchair from a bout with polio in 1950, played "air drums" on the arm of the sofa.

And when I grew up I played at clubs like Uncle Lennie had, and on baby grand pianos, after all, at private holiday parties where people draped themselves over the piano with Brie and champagne and sang "God Rest ye Merry Gentlemen." Once, I played all night in the club car of The Montrealer, on my way home from Baltimore to Vermont for Christmas, because the train was stuck in a snowdrift outside New Rochelle, New York. Accompanied by a student from Julliard on violin, I played while other people sang, one of them passing around a jug of Gallo burgundy. And the people in the train stranded next to ours could only look on, wistfully.

Cool, at Last

So, it's funny how things work out. Through all the incidents and accidents, the struggles to look right and do the right thing, I had at last found my own path, my own way, to be *cool*. And it had had nothing to do with the way I looked, or how much I weighed. It was by doing something that I loved. And it had been right there, at my fingertips, all along.